# Labour of Love

# Labour of Love

## Essays on Work

Paul Marshall
Edward Vanderkloet
Peter Nijkamp
Sander Griffioen
Harry Antonides

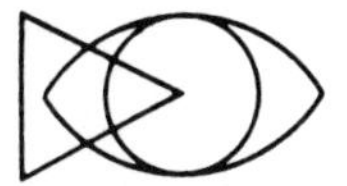

Wedge Publishing Foundation

Toronto

1980

Cover design: John Burnett, Toronto
Cover photograph: Courtesy of Nova Scotia Communications
and Information Centre
Typesetting: Printers Overload, Kitchener, Ontario
Printing: General Printers, Oshawa, Ontario

ISBN 0-88906-107-6

# Contents

# Introduction

This collection of essays is a sequel to *A Christian Union in Labour's Wasteland* published by Wedge in 1978. While both books proceed from the same outlook on modern society, their focus is different. The first publication found its origin in the history of the Christian Labour Association of Canada and contains essays written specifically in connection with the twenty-fifth anniversary of that body. Its orientation was practical and immediate, with an eye to the struggles of a small christian labour union in a quite hostile social environment. The present collection takes a certain distance from the immediate problems of unionism, and considers the issue of labour in the wider context of western society. The labour scene is explored in greater depth and from a variety of angles.

The essays in effect fall into two groups. The first three contributions are primarily of a historical nature. They pay attention to the place of work itself in the respective stages of western society, to the various theories of work, and to the valuations of work in human life. The last three essays deal with the future of labour in the light of the problems we have encountered in the past as well as the present. Griffioen's and Nijkamp's reveal the theoretical background of the authors. But the reflective character of their analyses only adds depth to their concrete suggestions. They also provide a background for Antonides's final chapter, which discusses alternative directions for concrete problems in industry.

There is no pretension here that the phenomenal problems of our highly industrialized societies are dealt with in an exhaustive manner. As a matter of fact, this little book shows that there are no easy answers to the vexing malformations in the western socioeconomies. Instead, the authors of the respective essays urgently suggest that Christians of evangelical conviction should be much more involved than they have been in the recent past with the concrete struggle in searching for new directions and more adequate solutions.

*Labour of Love* wants to contribute to a new sense of the meaning of work. If we are to find our way out of the impasse our daily occupations so often confront us with, work must again become an expression of love—to God and fellowmen.

*Josina Van Nuis Zylstra*
**Book editor**

# 1
# Vocation, Work, and Jobs

*by Paul Marshall*

## Introduction

The concept *vocation* is much used in christian circles, but is often little understood and even less examined. There is an impression that it has something to do with work, but there is also the suspicion that the sorts of work readily available in our society are a far cry from any genuine christian callings. Some tend to reject the world entirely while others assert that we should not question and must work in the situations in which providence has placed us.

In this study I hope to clarify some of the important issues in this area by examining, comparing, and analyzing some christian teachings on *vocation, work,* and *jobs*. I particularly wish to emphasize the uniqueness of the biblical view of work. Having compared and criticized various views, I will try to give some broad advice on how we should begin to understand what is implied in these three terms.

Before going any further, I would like to make some brief comments on terminology. By *job* I mean any work which earns money, whether that be wages, salary, or self-employed income. By *labour* I mean physical work. I cannot easily define what I mean by *work,* and I find most of the suggested definitions unsatisfactory. The sort of thing I have in mind is something similar to the popular understanding of work; it includes such things as one's job, or repairing the taps, or helping the kids with their homework, or making the bed. It would not include play, or sleeping, or eating, or relaxing, or contemplating, or certain types of prayer. What I mean by *vocation* will become clearer as the study progresses.

## The Bible and work

The late Hannah Arendt, otherwise one of the most penetrating commentators on the modern age, once voiced the opinion that "Christianity . . . never developed a positive labour philosophy."[1] A strange judgment from one so wise. Admittedly, she was considering principally the pre-Reformation period, but, even so, the statement was a sweeping one and tended to dismiss Protestantism (and later Roman Catholicism) out of hand. Admittedly also, she was thinking of physical labour, but in this her judgment was probably even more seriously awry.

But one needn't look just to Protestantism for a high view of work; the Bible is full of it. We will restrict our discussion to the New Testament, but we should note that in Genesis the curse was not the imposition of labour as such but only that labour would become harsh and painful; it is clear that work was considered one of the blessings before the fall. Even as far back as the time of Noah, Yahweh was graciously ameliorating some of the effects of this curse on work.[2]

In the New Testament we find a people immersed in the life and problems of working people. The apostles were mainly of humble background and sometimes returned to their work after being called by Jesus. Jesus was himself a carpenter for all but the last few years of his life. His parables referred to sowers (Matthew 13:3), vineyard labourers (Matthew 13:30), harvesters (John 4:35), house building (Matthew 7:24), swine tending (Luke 15:11), and women sweeping house (Luke 15:8).[3]

The apostle Paul never developed any systematic teaching on work, at least not that we know about. However, his writing contained a sustained polemic against idleness and he gave many exhortations on work.[4] He made no distinction between physical and spiritual work and used the same terms to refer to both the manual labour by which he earned a living and his apostolic service.[5] Often it is difficult to know to which he was referring. For him all the different types of work originated in faith. The work he considered was not limited to liberal pursuits; in fact, it was manual labour which most often drew his attention. When he outlined the service of the "new man . . . created after the likeness of God," he urged him to "do good work with his hands." Paul himself worked with his hands so as not to be a burden to the church. In fact, this highly educated man worked with his own hands to support others, and he urged the practice on other Christians.[6]

Paul's advice to slaves, that they should work willingly as they were the slaves of Christ, illustrates the same theme. It did not mean that Paul uncritically accepted the institution of slavery but it shows that he in no way looked down on the work of the slave; rather, he regarded even slave labour as service to the Lord on a par with his own work. His position was summarized in his remarkable declaration "There is neither . . . slave nor free . . . you are all one in Christ Jesus."[7]

Similarly with Paul's often quoted and misunderstood declaration "if anyone does not work, let him not eat," which was not an expression of callousness toward those who could not support themselves; the complex early church system of deacons, collections for the poor, and sharing of goods shows that this was not the case. Paul was concerned not with those who could not find work, but with those who could and yet refused to share the burdens of their fellows. He was asserting that a life of leisure or one solely devoted to religious contemplation was a deficient life—that all members of the church should be involved in useful activity.[8]


## The ancient world and work

Probably we are familiar with some of the ideas just outlined, and they may even seem rather old hat. But when the biblical teaching is compared with the attitudes toward work of the educated in the Greek and Roman world, then it appears novel, startling, and quite electrifying. Most of the examples we have are from those who were more philosophically inclined; there isn't too much of a record from the ones who actually did most of the work.[9] Given this restriction, it is clear that the educated viewed what we now call work with some disdain, a disdain which extended toward those who were involved in such work.

One type of work which drew widespread condemnation was that of the artisan. Xenophon put the words in Socrates' mouth that "the illiberal arts (banausikai), as they are called, are spoken against, and are, naturally enough, held in utter disdain in our states . . . [they] . . . leave no spare time for attention to one's friends and the city . . . . In fact, in some of the states, it is not even lawful for any of the citizens to work at illiberal arts."[10] Aristotle asked that citizens cultivate leisure, as "leisure is a necessity, both for growth in goodness and for the pursuit of political activities."[11] Isocrates held that citizenship rights should be restricted to those "who could afford the time and possessed sufficient means."[12] Later, Cicero used the term *sordidi* to describe the occupation of artisans, while the writers at the end of the Roman Republic had an ideal of *otium* (leisure) *cum dignitate.*[13]

At times there appeared to be something of a different view concerning those involved in agriculture. Xenophon thought that "even stouthearted warriors cannot live without the aid of workers . . . those who stock and cultivate the land"; Aristotle thought that the "best kind of populace is one of farmers"; Cicero thought that "none is better than agriculture . . . none more becoming in a free man."[14]

The reason for this duality is contained in Cicero's qualifier "in a free man." The idea of doing something with one's hands was not itself necessarily degrading. Even Homer's Odysseus could build his own boat and Penelope could spin and weave; Paris of Troy helped build his own house while Nausicäa did her brothers' laundry.[15] But this type of activity was freely chosen; it was independent. What was objected to was work and relations based on dependency and necessity—the absence of autonomy (*autarkeia*). Freedom at the time of Aristotle consisted of "status, personal inviolability, freedom of economic activity and right of unrestricted movement."[16] The slaves, the majority of the population, lacked all of these, and the artisans, while under contract, lacked the last two for a limited time. Hence

Aristotle thought that craftsmen were really part slaves, and therefore a bit less than fully human. In his list of "ways of life," he did not even bother to mention the craftsmen because it was obvious to him that such people were not free.[17]

This concern with absence of necessity carried over into attitudes toward farming. Aristotle ranked shepherds high because "The laziest are shepherds; for they get their food without labour (*ponos*) from tame animals and have leisure (*skholazousin*)."[18] Hesiod, the poet, praised farming, but he advised his brother "Make haste, you and your slaves alike . . . set your slaves to winnow Demeter's holy grain . . . put your bondman out of doors and look out for a servant girl with no children . . . let your men rest their poor knees."[19] No poor peasant this who must do his own work! Those who praised agriculture assumed that the actual farm labour was being done by slaves and servants. Their praise was for the landowner as the backbone of the political order.

## A comparison of Paul and Seneca

The only exceptions to this sort of view occurred in the stoic philosophers. Chryssipus reversed Aristotle's treatment of the servant in terms of the slave and he considered slaves in the light of servants. He held that slaves were merely hired for life and that their rights were violated if they were actually possessed by the master. Stoic philosophy gave work a value of its own and held that it did not exclude one from a virtuous life.[20]

Despite this similarity, it is clear that many of the parallels between Christianity and stoicism have been badly overstated. We will try to show this by a brief comparison of Paul and Seneca. Seneca was a contemporary of Paul; indeed some scholars think they may even have met while Paul was in Rome. He was quite similar to Paul in some respects and Calvin's first work was a commentary on his *De Clementia*.

However, Seneca tended to view the person as composed of two different things—body and soul, and the soul was definitely higher; "What else could you call such a soul than a God dwelling in a human body (*deus in corpore humans hospitans*)?" In this dualism the body was certainly essential; Seneca confessed to "an inborn affection for our body . . . we should cherish the body with great care." Nevertheless the body was "to be regarded as *necessary* rather than important." Seneca saw the soul residing in the body as beneath a heavy burden (*gravis sarcina*); the body was a weight and a penance (*pondus ac poena*), chains (*in vinculis*) and a prison (*carcer*). In fact, he held that "To despise our bodies is pure freedom" (*contemptus corporis sui certa libertas est*).[21]

In contrast to this, Paul emphasized that the resurrection was the resurrection of the *body*. He held that the body was not a prison, but the *temple* of the Holy Spirit; in fact he usually used the expression "your bodies" in such a way that it meant "yourselves." For Paul "spirit" (*pneuma*) was never a distinct *part* of man and the best translation of *psyche* in his writings is probably "life." The war between "flesh" and "spirit" was not a war between body and soul, but between tendencies to obedience and disobedience.[22]

These two different views of mankind gave rise to two different views of work. Seneca certainly thought that nobility of mind could be found in all classes, for "Socrates was no aristocrat. Cleanthes worked at a well and served as a hired man watering a garden. Philosophy did not find Plato a nobleman; it made him one." Everyone could enter the "households . . . of noblest intellects." But, in his scheme, this only meant that such work was not a barrier to the higher life. Philosophical activity was still the best sort of life; Seneca was only saying that all sorts of people could enter now into it. In fact, he thought that the "common sort" of arts were "concerned with equipping life; there is in them no pretence to beauty or honour."[23] Such a view was in marked contrast to Paul, who viewed all types of work, mental or physical, as potentially equal service to the Lord.

## *Pre-Reformation Christianity*

We have compared the New Testament with other ancient views rather extensively in order to doubly emphasize the Bible's distinctiveness. Even compared to the stoic philosophers, who were the most generous in their appraisal of necessary work, the biblical authors stand out starkly in their

praise of even the humblest honest labour. The Bible was a
radical document in respect to work.

Over the centuries the biblical motifs were overshadowed by
other concerns. We cannot hope to do justice to all of these
developments, so we will focus just on two of the most
important figures—Augustine and Thomas Aquinas.

Augustine sought to come to grips with the entire life of the
world about him as he sought to understand the relationship of
the City of God to the City of Man. He had praise for the work of
farmers, craftsmen, and even, on occasion, for merchants. He
certainly thought that "Christians will not refuse the discipline
of this temporal life." However, he tended to view this life as
only a *school* for life eternal. One analogy he used was that of a
wayside inn, "Thou art passing on the journey thou hast begun,
thou hast come, again to depart, not to abide . . . this life is but
a wayside inn. Use [it] . . . with the purpose not of remaining
but of leaving them behind." In this conception, one could
"use" (*uti*) worldly goods, but one could "enjoy" (*frui*) spiritual
goods.[24]

Augustine distinguished between an "active life" (*vita activa*)
and a "contemplative life" (*vita contemplativa*). The
contemplative life was akin to Aristotle's *bios politikois* and was
largely derived from Greek and Roman thinking. The *vita activa*
took in almost every kind of work, even including that of
studying, preaching, and teaching, while the *vita contemplativa*
was reflection and meditation upon God and his truth. While
both of these kinds of life were good, the contemplative life was
of a higher order. At times it might be necessary for one to have
the active life, but, wherever possible, one should choose the
other; "the one life is loved, the other endured." "The
obligations of charity make us undertake righteous business
(*negotium*)" but "If no one lays this burden upon us, we should
give ourselves up to leisure (*otium*) to the perception and
contemplation of truth."[25]

Thomas Aquinas also took the world and all its work with the
utmost seriousness. He was a member of a largely urban order,
the Dominicans, and he sought to come to grips with all the
manifestations of life about him, to point out the place of each
human concern in the overarching of God's creation. For him
the division of labour was a manifestation that all were the

members of the one body; he even compared God to a master craftsman.[26]

However, Thomas also used Augustine's distinction of the *vita contemplativa* and the *vita activa*. Although he gave everything its place, yet some things had a higher place than others. The *vita contemplativa* was "oriented to the eternal" whereas the *vita activa* was only because of the "necessities of the present life." The active life was connected only to the needs of the human body that men and animals had in common. It was good if it was necessary but if one could stay alive without such work, then so much the better; it might even function only as a last resort. While both lives had their place, the active life was bound by necessity and only the contemplative life was truly free. In short, "the life of contemplation" was "simply better than the life of action."[27]

This sort of distinction formed the basic pattern of medieval Christianity. It resulted in a conception according to which the only true christian calling, or, at least, the highest calling, was a priestly or monastic one. In fact the term *calling* or *vocation* was only used to refer to such pursuits. Karl Barth's summary was quite accurate:

> According to the view prevalent at the height of the high Middle ages [secular work] only existed to free for the work of their profession those who were totally and exclusively occupied in rendering true obedience for the salvation of each and all. There could be no question of "calling" for Christians in other professions.[28]

There were exceptions to this trend, the German mystics Meister Eckhart and Johann Tauler, and the English John Wyclif being the prime examples.[29] But each of these figures was regarded as mildly or outrightly heretical. Their unorthodox stance merely serves to throw into sharper focus the prevailing ethos of medieval Christianity.


## The Reformation and work

In the Reformation there was a very different outlook from the then existing Roman Catholic one. Almost without exception the Reformers maintained that all forms of work were of equal value and were equally pleasing to God. Indeed, one of the articles of heresy against William Tyndale, the major English Reformer, who was executed for heresy in 1536, was that he taught "There is no work better than another to please God; to pour water, to wash dishes, to be a souter (cobbler), or an apostle, all is one; to wash dishes and to preach is all one, as touching the deed, to please God." Tyndale was of the opinion that "In Christ we are all of one degree, without respect of persons." His fellow Reformer John Frith, executed in 1533, was of the same opinion:

> How shalt thou learn to understand the Scripture, than by going about to fulfill that thou there readest? And if thou go about to fulfill it . . . then thou must work with thy hands, for that doth St. Paul teach thee.[30]

The same views were the theme of the continental Reformation teaching. Luther taught that God in his providence had put every person in his place in society to do the work of that place:

> If you are a manual laborer, you find that the Bible has been put into your workshop, into your hand, into your heart. It teaches and preaches how you should treat your neighbour . . . just look at your tools . . . at your needle and thimble, your beer barrel, your goods, your scales or yardstick or measure . . . and you will read this statement inscribed in them. Everywhere you look, it stares at you . . . . You have as many preachers as you have transactions, goods, tools and other equipment in your house and home.

Even Adam had "work to do, that is . . . plant the garden, cultivate and look after it." "Everything our bodies do, the external and the carnal, is and is called spiritual behaviour, if God's word is added to it and it is done in faith. There is therefore nothing which is so bodily, carnal and external that it does not become spiritual when it is done in the Word of God and faith." Luther's wicked jibe at the humanist Erasmus that he had no real sympathy with God's good creation and stared at the creatures "as a cow stares at a new gate" may not say much about Luther's knowledge of Erasmus, but speaks volumes about his knowledge of cows![31]

Calvin was perhaps the strongest in his exhortations on work. Above all, he stressed *useful* work; his God was "not such as is imagined by the Sophists, vain, idle and almost asleep, but vigilant, efficacious, operative, and engaged in continual action." In his commentary on the parable of the talents (Luke 19:11-27), he broke away from previous interpretations which had understood the "talents" as spiritual gifts and graces. Calvin related the talents to everyday work and calling; the particular example he considered was trading *(negotiara)*. He stressed the concrete nature of these gifts and helped shape the modern meaning of the word *talent*. André Biéler, in his classic work on Calvin's social views, described Calvin's position thus:

> Companionship is completed in work and in the interplay of economic exchanges. Human fellowship is realized in relationships which flow from the division of labour wherein each person has been called of God to a particular and partial work which complements the work of others. The mutual exchange of goods and services is the concrete sign of the profound solidarity which unites humanity.[32]

There were certainly errors in the Reformers' views, as we shall see below, but the general pattern of their teaching was essentially that of the New Testament: All work is equal in value; all our work is to be service to God; when done before the face of God, this world with its duties is our sphere of service.

It is hard to escape the impression that the followers of Augustine and Aquinas were to serve in the world only when necessary, that Luther's followers were ushered out to serve in the world, and that Calvin's followers were let loose to transform the world.

As in the case of the biblical doctrines, it should be stressed that this teaching was distinctive, indeed unique. We have already covered some of the Roman Catholic views (which continued through Reformation times) so we can emphasize this distinctiveness by a comparison with the other major renewal movement of the day—the Renaissance.

## The Renaissance and work

Renaissance figures shared with the Reformers a desire to remould people's attitudes to the world; they too altered conceptions of the rather fruitless duality of the *vita activa* and the *vita contemplativa.* However, the suggestions they made were quite different from those of the Reformers. In considering the humanists, we will restrict our brief survey to English developments.

Perhaps the first thing one notes on reading the humanists' writings is their leisured and irenic tone—a far cry from the often earthy, hasty and, at times, almost grubby tones of the English Reformers. Saint Thomas More's *Utopia,* while a delight to read, is very difficult to understand because of its ironic tone and oblique message. However, certain things are clear; according to More, "the main purpose of [the Utopian's] whole economy is to give persons . . . free time from physical drudgery . . . so that they can cultivate the mind—which they regard as the secret of a happy life."[33]

More's friend and coworker, Thomas Lupset, lecturer in rhetoric at Oxford, took a stoic view. He sought the

> rest that angels in heaven have . . . none other but this, not to be moved or stirred with these passions, of loving, of hating, of being pleased, of being diseased, of trusting, of lusting, of abhorring, of coveting, of refusing, of rejoicing, of lamenting, of innumerable such other, that scoureth and shippeth man's mind by reason of the corrupt affection and love that he beareth in his itching body.

Lupset thought that "our spirit and our mind only hath things that truly be called goods." Another friend and member of More's circle, Thomas Starkey, chaplain to Henry VIII, held that "high philosophy and contemplation of nature be of itself a greater perfection of man's mind . . . ."[34]

Despite this praise for rest, philosophy, and contemplation, the humanists did not despise an active life. In fact, Lupset's main point was to urge involvement with the affairs of the commonwealth, for

> . . . the meddling with the causes of the commonweal is more necessary and ever rather and first to be chosen, as the principal mean whereby we may attain to the other [i.e. contemplation].[35]

They stressed again and again that the educated should be politically responsible and they thought that no other form of life would be possible if men did not bend their efforts to secure an ordered commonwealth. However, they still viewed this work only as *necessary;* it was required in order to facilitate the higher realm of freedom and contemplation. The way they placed contemplation and action in the structure of their thought was not substantially different from that of Augustine or Aquinas.

Another difference between the humanists and the Reformers was in the types of action they actually considered. The evangelical works were full of dishes, spades, ploughs, tools and trading, but the Renaissance writing touched almost exclusively on political action, the task of an elite. The ideal humanist was an educated, pious, cultured gentleman and advisor; the life of action was that of the wise counselor to the prince. The protestant pattern of reform was to call each and every person to his duty, but the humanist pattern was one of the education of the ruler and the elevation of the wise and virtuous to positions of authority, a pattern the humanists themselves exemplified in their appointments as secretaries and ambassadors.

## *The Reformers' confusion of vocation, work, and job*

While we have stressed the distinctiveness of the Reformation teaching on work and have maintained that the substance of what they taught was essentially biblical, it should not be thought that their views were without spot or wrinkle. In fact, many of our present problems stem from some of the Reformers' mistakes. I would like just to focus on one point, to wit: the confusion of vocation, work, and job.

One of the key texts in the Reformers' understanding of work was I Corinthians 7:20: "Abide in the calling in which you were called." Almost without exception they took the "calling" in this text to mean the works and estates that Christians were already in. Hence they taught that all persons should accept the place and station in society that they were in as the sphere where God had commanded them to work—in short, it was their calling. Luther often interchanged calling and social station (*Stand*). While Calvin was more open to changing work, he usually advised people to stay put unless they had "good grounds" and, hence, clearly related calling or vocation to a christian's place in the social order and the economic division of labour.

Such an interpretation was a misreading of Paul unless he was using the word "calling" *(klesis)* in a sense used nowhere else in his or any other Greek writings. It seems most likely that Paul was saying that circumcision or uncircumcision was relatively unimportant (vv. 17-19), that one's type of work was relatively unimportant (vv. 21-24), and that what was paramount was that people abide in the calling *as Christians.*

When the Reformers filtered their understanding of work through their interpretation of this text, they sidetracked the biblical theme. A calling tended to be reduced to the activities required by being in a particular place in society. Thus to be a cobbler, a housewife, a husband, a preacher, or a farmer was a calling. Obedience in the world was focused in a particular type of work for each person.[36] The overall result of this was that Christians were directed to serve God in the world, but the world and its "callings" were taken for granted. The renewing implications of christian vocation were suppressed in favour of a quiescence and passivity before the social order. Christians were to be farmers, housewives, and merchants, but never really asked whether being such was really such a fruitful and just service under the prevailing conditions.

Over the next 150 years, with the growth of *jobs* (i.e., paid work), the idea of calling became even narrower. Calling then tended to mean just a type of *job.* One result of this was that unpaid work was downgraded. "Real" work was paid; activities like comforting the heartbroken or visiting the sick were all right, but they were a bit lightweight if they didn't bring in the bacon. Women still had something of a vocation in housekeeping and parenting, but that was somehow not up to par with "real" work. Men's vocations were their jobs, trades, and professions; other things might be good but were, with the exception of piety, optional.

Another result of the fact that a calling *was* a job was that, as work structures changed, the content of a calling changed as well. To be sure, Christians were urged to be honest and earnest, but the actual *content* of the work they were doing was never open to question. This eventually resulted in the sort of teaching offered by the late seventeenth-century Puritan, Richard Steele,

> let (a man) be never so active out of his sphere, he will be at a great loss, if he do not keep his own vineyard and mind his own business . . . it is not our sin that we do not supply another's negligence, by doing that which belongs not in our place . . . there is poor comfort in suffering for doing that which was not the work of our place and calling . . . .[37]

The general maxims of an individualistic and secularizing age now provided almost the sole content of a christian calling. While it is true that such a tendency was not developed in the Reformers themselves, they sowed the seeds which ultimately grew up and almost strangled any biblical conception of vocation.

## Barth and Ellul on vocation

What can we do with this misidentification of calling with job or profession, the urging that we find our place in the social and economic order and do what it requires, albeit honestly and with integrity? One solution has been suggested by Karl Barth and, following him, Jacques Ellul.

In what is probably the greatest discussion of vocation in modern theology, Barth was the first to point out how Protestantism had accepted the givens of the secular world in its doctrine of calling. He asked:

> Does not this once again bind man's obedience to a law which is different from the calling itself, except that now this is the law of the world and its historical and transitory order instead of that of the cloister? Ought not the divine calling and man's obedience necessarily entail the transformation and new definition and form of the sphere of operation?

Barth's questions went to the heart of the matter. However, as a reaction to previous mistakes, he tended to divorce vocation from this creation altogether. He related it only to the coming of God's Kingdom, which he saw as something almost completely unrelated to God's created order. Jacques Ellul has taken the same track and, borrowing from Marx, relates *work* to the *necessity* of this world, as distinct from *vocation* which he relates to the freedom of the coming Kingdom. Ellul hence refuses to relate vocation to one's job or occupation; in fact, he appears to take it out of this world altogether. A similar tendency was present in Barth, who thought that "faithfulness in vocation must exclude any intention of radically reforming life." Ellul goes so far as to say that even the work of the caring social worker seeking to bring genuine healing cannot be called "christian." For him, the work of this world, the work of necessity, is of a lower order; the work of freedom, oriented to a future Kingdom with no roots in this creation, is the only truly "christian" task. Here we have Augustine and Aquinas, or even Seneca and Aristotle, in new garb. Although different in intent, the position is not too different in substance from that of the fundamentalist who only accepts work in the "world" for income in order to allow the true obedience of evangelism and piety.[38]

Hence, while we can applaud Barth and Ellul for revealing the unbiblical elements in much of the protestant teaching on vocation, we must reject their solution as one which downplays God's creation and the reasons why humankind was created in the first place.


## Some suggestions on vocation and work

What can we say then? Well, firstly, Genesis teaches us that we were created to honour, love, and enjoy God, and to tend and bring out the fruitfulness of his creation (Genesis 1:26-31). But, through our sin, the creation is fallen. We have acted disobediently and erected structures and economies shaped in sin, whose practices and results may be awful, no matter what the honesty or diligence with which a Christian, or any other, serves in them. Even the ground is cursed and unruly. We know that we need to be redeemed from this condition.

Doesn't the fall mean that this creation can no longer be a proper sphere of obedience? By no means! Paul teaches us that it was through Christ that the world was made, that even now it is Christ who upholds the world, and that through Christ the whole creation will be redeemed, "all things in heaven and earth" (Colossians 1:13-20). Redemption is not the negation of creation but its *renewal!*

In Christ we and the whole creation will be restored and *are being* restored to perform those tasks and fulfil those relationships we were created and fitted for. Already in Genesis, Yahweh brought succour from the effects of sin (Genesis 3:21; 4:1, 15; 5:29; 8:15-9:7). We do not flee the world, for our sin does not replace the world, but only distorts it. *Even sinfully, we can only act in the order God has put us in and which Christ upholds.* Our calling is to obediently serve in the healing, renewing, and unfolding of God's good creation; to love God, to live before his face in praying, raising children, doing justice, making chairs, building, playing, eating, sleeping; to do all things to his honour and glory. In doing this, we need to distinguish between those things which are the result of sin and those which reflect God's good creation, no matter how broken.

Within all this, work and employment have a place, even though they are not the totality of our vocation. We must seek to serve in ways that, in the light of justice and stewardship, will bring genuine healing. This can mean refusing to work in building nuclear plants, even as a cook, or refusing to advertise electric toothbrushes or potato chips. It can mean breaking out of the mores and arrogance of a profession (Bernard Shaw defined a profession as "a conspiracy against the laity"), or erecting new structures and economic organizations altogether. It could also mean taking almost anything just to bring money in, if that is what is necessary. Many people don't have much of a choice, but certainly the growth of christian community and mutual support will enable more of us to take up truly stewardly work. The sort of work we are to do is never something that can be decided abstractly and in isolation; it depends on the whole state of the polity, society, and economy we live in. We can never take this world for granted, but we must seek to reform it through all our actions.

One final word—we are not to be obsessed with work. Our vocation is not in the first place to do a particular task, but to be christian in all our relationships in God's creation. This means, among other things, that we are called to rest, a fact that Protestantism, particularly Calvinism, has continually underplayed. I never fail to be amused by the fact that on the seventh day "God rested from all the work he had done." If God can take a rest, why on earth can't we?

*Notes*

1.     Hannah Arendt, *The Human Condition* (New York: Doubleday, 1959), p. 290.

2.     See Genesis 3:17-19; 4:28-29. On one of the possible means of the ameliorating of the harshness of work, compare Genesis 1:28-30 with Genesis 9:1-7. On Old Testament views see Alan Richardson, *The Biblical Doctrine of Work* (London: S.C.M., 1958); A.T. Geoghegan, *The Attitude Toward Labour in Early Christianity and Ancient Culture* (Washington: Catholic University of America Press, 1945), pp. 47-64.

3.     See also Matthew 9:34; 10:10; Luke 10:7.

4.     Cf. II Thessalonians 3:6; Richardson, *Biblical Doctrine of Work*, pp. 57 ff.; E. Gryglewicz, "La valeur du travail manuel dans la terminologie grecque de la bible," *Biblica,* vol. 7 (1965), pp. 314-337; J.N. Sevenster, *Paul and Seneca* (Leiden: E.J. Brill, 1961), pp.211ff.

5.     Cf. I Corinthians 4:12; 15:10; 16:16; Ephesians 4:28; Romans 16:12; Galatians 4:11; Philippians 2:16; Colossians 1:29; I Thessalonians 5:12.

6.     Ephesians 4:17-32, esp. v. 28; II Corinthians 11:9; 12:13; II Thessalonians 3:8; I Thessalonians 4:9-12; Acts 20:35.

7.     Ephesians 6:6,7; Galatians 3:28. Paul's statements appear to contradict Arendt's statements that he recommended labour only "as a good means to stay out of trouble." Arendt, *Human Condition*, p. 289.

8.     II Thessalonians 3:10. See also Matthew 9:34; 10:10; Luke 10:7.

9.     On the attitude of those actually engaged in the work, see Geoghegan, *Attitude Toward Labour,* pp. 48-54.

10.     *Oeconomicus* IV: 2, 3; Claud Mossé, *The Ancient World at Work* (London: Chatto and Windus, 1969), p. 25. See also Pierre Jacard, *Histoire sociale du travail* (Paris: Payot, 1960), pp. 66-75.

11.     *Politics* 1329a, 1-2.

12.     *Areopagitica* 26.

13.     *De officiis* I: 42, 150; Mossé, *Ancient World at Work*, p. 25.

14.     *Oeconomicus* IV: 15; *Politics* 1318b, 1; *De officiis* I, 42. See also Alison Burford, *Craftsmen in Greek and Roman Society* (London: Thames and Hudson, 1972), esp. pp. 29-30 on Cicero's attitude to farmers; Geoghegan, *Attitude Toward Labour,* pp. 37-38.

15.     Arendt, *Human Condition*, p. 290.

16.     W. Westerman, "Between Slavery and Freedom," *American Historical Review,* vol. 50 (1945), pp. 213-227. See also E.G. Kaiser, *Theology of Work* (Westminster, Maryland: Newman Press, 1966), pp. 32ff.

17.     *Nichomachaean Ethics* I:5; *Eudaemonian Ethics* 1215a, 35f; *Politics* 1337b, 5; Arendt, *Human Condition*, p. 302; R. Schlaifer, "Greek Theories of

Slavery from Homer to Aristotle," *Harvard Studies in Classical Philology*, vol. 47 (1936), pp. 165-204.

18.    *Politics* 1256a, 30f. Aristotle equated *skhole* and *aergia,* leisure and laziness. Cf. Arendt, *Human Condition*, pp. 323-324.

19.    *Works'and Days* 1, 383-617.

20.    Ludwig Edelstein, *The Meaning of Stoicism* (Cambridge: Cambridge University Press, 1966), pp. 74-78.

21.    Sevenster, *Paul and Seneca,* pp. 69, 72; *Epistolae* 14, 1, 2; 23, 6; 24, 17; 31, 11; 62, 22; 76, 25; 79, 12; 92, 33; *De consolatione ad Helvian* 11, 6.

22.    I Corinthians 6:15, 19, 20; 12:27; 15: 44, 50; Romans 6:13; Philippians 3:21; Sevenster, *Paul and Seneca,* pp. 77-81; Jacard, *Histoire sociale du travail,* pp. 102-112.

23.    *Epistolae* 31, 4-5; 44, 1-4; *De brevitate vitae* 15, 3. See also *Epistolae* 88, 20, 28; 89, 13; Sevenster, *Paul and Seneca,* p. 215.

24.    *De civitate dei* I, 29; XI, 25; Herbert A. Deane, *The Political and Social Ideas of St. Augustine* (New York: Columbia University Press, 1963), pp. 44, 108ff.

25.    Dom Cuthbert Butler, *Western Mysticism* (New York: Barnes and Noble, 1968), pp. 157-165; Arendt, *Human Condition*, pp. 13, 15, 304, 376-377; "Sermon" CLXIX, 17; *De civitate dei* XI, 16; XIX, 1, 2, 19; *Expositio in Psalmos* 69, 7; *In Ioann. Evangel.* 6, 25-26; *Tract in Ioann.* CXXIV, 5.

26.    Cf. G. O'Brien, *An Essay on Medieval Economic Thinking* (London: Longmans, Green, 1920), p. 129; S.M. Killeen, *The Philosophy of Labour According to Thomas Aquinas* (Washington: Catholic University of America Press, 1939).

27.    *Summa theologiae* ii. 2. 179; ii. 2, 181. 1-4; ii. 2. 182. 1, 2; *Expositio in Psalmos* 45. 3; *Summa contra gentiles* iii. 135; Arendt, *Human Condition,* pp. 290, 303-304, 377.

28.    Karl Barth, "Vocation," pp. 600ff. of vol. 3, part 4 of his *Church Dogmatics,* trans. A.T. Mackay, T.H.L. Parker, H. Knight, H.A. Kennedy, J. Marks (Edinburgh: T. and T. Clark, 1961), p. 602; Th. Scharmann, G. Mensching, F. Lau, W. Freytag, W. Nordmann, J. Fichtner, "Beruf" in *Die Religion in Geschichte und Gegenwart,* ed. J.C.B. Mohr (Tübingen: J.C.B. Mohr, 1957), pp. 1071-1080, 1078; K. Holl, "Die Geschichte des Worts 'Beruf'" in his *Gesammelte Aufsätze zur Kirchengeschichte,* vol. 3 (Tübingen: J.C.B. Mohr, 1931), pp. 184-219, pp. 199f.

29.    For Eckhart, see R.C. Petry, ed., *Late Medieval Mysticism* (Philadelphia: Westminster Press, 1957), pp. 193-199; for Tauler, see *Oeuvres complètes,* 9 vols. (Paris: Tralin, 1911), vol. 3, pp. 454-464, vol. 4, pp. 126-147; for Wyclif, see *Select English Works,* 3 vols. (Oxford: Oxford University Press, 1871), vol. 3, pp. 130-134, 142-143, 148f.

30.    William Tyndale, "A Parable of the Wicked Mammon" (1527) in *Doctrinal Treatises and Portions of Holy Scripture* (Cambridge: Parker Society,

1848), pp. 98, 104; W.R. Jones, *The Tudor Commonwealth, 1529-1559* (London: Athlone Press, 1970), p. 68.

31.	Gustav Wingren, *Luther on Vocation* (Philadelphia: Muhlenberg Press, 1957), pp. 70-72; Paul Althaus, *The Ethics of Martin Luther* (Philadelphia: Muhlenberg Press, 1972), pp. 40, 101. *Luther's Works* (Philadelphia and St. Louis: Concordia and Muhlenberg, 1955- ), vol. 21, p. 237; vol. 31, p. 360.

32.	*Institutes* I. 16. 3; Mario Miegge, *I Talenti Messi a Profitto* (Urbino: Argalia, 1969), pp. 7, 112-113; André Biéler, *La pensée économique et sociale de Calvin* (Geneva: Librairie de l'Université, 1961), p. 321.

33.	Thomas More, *Utopia* (London: Pelican, 1965), p. 76.

34.	Thomas Lupset, "A Treatise of Charity" (1533), pp. 207-231 of J.A. Gee, *Life and Works of Thomas Lupset* (New Haven: Yale University Press, 1928), pp. 212-213; "An Exhortation to Young Men," pp. 235-262 of Gee, *Life and Works of Lupset*, p. 258; see also Lupset's "A Treatise of Dying Well" (1534), pp. 265-290 of Gee, *Life and Works of Lupset*, pp. 270-277.

35.	Thomas Starkey, *A Dialogue Between Pole and Lupset* (London: Chatto and Windus, 1948), pp. 25f. See also Fritz Caspari, *Humanism and the Social Order in England* (Chicago: University of Chicago Press, 1954), pp. 121-122. The humanist stress on political activity is one of the principal themes of vol. 1 of Quentin Skinner's *The Foundations of Modern Political Thought*, 2 vols. (Cambridge: Cambridge University Press, 1978).

36.	Cf. Wingren, *Luther on Vocation*, p. 64; *Calvin's Commentary on the First Epistle to the Corinthians* (Grand Rapids: Eerdmans, 1960), pp. 150-155; *Institutes* 3. 10. 6.

37.	I have traced the post-Reformation evolution of calling as job in "The Calling: Secularization and Economics in the Seventeenth Century," paper presented at the *Annual Meeting of the Canadian Political Science Association*, London, Ontario, 1978, and in "John Locke: Between God and Mammon," *Canadian Journal of Political Science*, vol. 12 (1979), pp. 73-96.

38.	Barth, "Vocation," vol. 3, part 4 of his *Church Dogmatics*, pp. 641-642, 644-645; compare Emil Brunner, *The Divine Imperative* (London: Lutterworth, 1937), pp. 200-228. For Ellul, see his "Work and Calling," *Katallagete*, Fall/Winter 1972. Ellul's position is summarized usefully by Vernard Eller in *The Reformed Journal*, May 1979, pp. 16-21. Nicholas Wolterstorff's reply to Eller in *The Reformed Journal*, May 1979, pp. 20-23 is an excellent statement on vocation. For Marx on freedom and necessity, see Erich Fromm's "Foreword," pp. i-vi, and also pp. vii-xi of Karl Marx, *Early Writings*, ed. T.B. Bottomore (New York: McGraw-Hill, 1964).

# 2
# *Why Work Anyway?* [*]

*by Edward Vanderkloet*

The search for a theory of labour and labour relations in the Bible is as futile as the attempt to find in it a theory about the origins of the earth. The Bible does not speak about labour as such; in fact, it doesn't speak about anything *as such*. It tells us who God is—Creator and Redeemer—and it tells us about man and his task as God's trustee in creation. In Genesis 3 labour is not cursed but man the mismanager, and this curse will show itself in his labour as well as in all other aspects of his life. But the lifting of the curse by Jesus Christ also means that life and labour will again become a joy and a blessing, if man responds to God's call to obedience.

From the outset I wish to remove a possible misunderstanding. There are many Christians who readily agree that man can only find joy in his daily work if he lives out of Christ's liberation, but also insist that a Christian can be happy in his daily work no matter what that work may be. Such people have localized sin and restricted it to the human heart without

---

realizing the corrupting power of that sin in all human relations and structures. This reductionism not only minimizes the power of sin; it also makes a caricature of Christ's redemption. People who hold such a view are often a stumbling block on the road to renewal. My plea for a restructuring of work does not spring from the belief that this will bring about shalom, for shalom is a gift of God. But shalom needs to be experienced in our relationships with others, and it is precisely our work relationships which frequently prevent that. When Paul admonishes slaves to be obedient to their masters, he does not condone slavery. He only urges Christ-believers to be examples of christian love. At the same time he reminds masters and servants alike that they have a heavenly employer who makes no distinction between master and servant.


## The ancient world

The Greeks and Romans generally despised work and idealized leisure. Didn't the gods spend their time eating, drinking, and being merry, and did they not punish a man (Sisyphus) by making him work? In Greek as well as in Latin, work was called *unleisure*. Aristotle wrote in his *Politics:* "in the best-governed polis . . . the citizens may not lead either the life of craftsmen or of traders, for such a life is devoid of nobility and hostile to perfection of character."[1] During the fifth century before Christ, the government of the Greek city of Thebes issued a decree prohibiting the citizens from engaging in work. And Plato taught that the highest classes of society should devote themselves to philosophy and the arts of thinking and governing, the middle classes should spend their time on sports and military matters, whereas the lowest classes should engage in work. Cicero, the great Roman lawyer who lived just before the beginning of the christian era, stated: "The toil of a hired worker, who is paid only for his toil and not for artistic skill is unworthy of a free man and is sordid in character . . . . Sordid too is the calling of those who buy wholesale in order to sell retail, since they would gain no profits without a great deal of lying."[2] The freemen in Athens and Rome engaged in sports, plays, war, philosophy, and art, while work was mostly done by slaves. Eighty percent of the Greek city states' population consisted of slaves, and the economy of the Roman empire, similarly, rested on a system of slavery. The collapse of Rome in the fifth century heralded the "Dark Ages" and plunged Europe into savagery. During the eighth and the ninth centuries, however, Christianity conquered the savage tribes that populated Spain, France, Britain, the Lowlands and Germany. Driven by new beliefs and a new work ethic during the high and late Middle Ages, the whole of western Europe was colonized and cultivated, requiring enormous activity on the part of the population. Spearheaded by monks, the land was deforested, large tracts were captured from the sea, and commercial cities and trading centres began to flourish.

The church was the first institution to stress the importance of manual labour. This applied especially to agricultural work but also held for craftsmanship. However, the church distinguished between three types of human activity. The spiritual work performed by the clergy, especially prayer, fasting and the giving of alms, was most important. Less exalted, yet highly honoured, was the work of the peasants and craftsmen. The third category pertained to the work of merchants and financiers, which, though necessary, was generally considered sinful. Usury and interest were forbidden and the making of profits was severely restricted. Christians should really not engage in such work; it should be limited to Jews and gentiles. (It is, by the way, no coincidence that ever since that time Jews have occupied the centres of power in the fields of trade and finance.)

Work relationships, like all human relationships, naturally reflect the prevailing notions about man and his place and task in the world. Medieval society was an autocratic and hierarchic one. The clergy occupied the highest rung of the social ladder; next came princes and noblemen; these were followed by craftsmen and peasants. Merchants and bankers were considered the scum of the earth. (Nevertheless, popes and kings did not hesitate to borrow heavily from these outcasts!) Authority was absolute and society was a caste system in which equal rights for all was an unknown concept. The unwholesome division of work stemmed from an unchristian concept of man's task in the world. So-called religious work and manual labour were considered God-pleasing, whereas the rest of human activity was seen as an inevitable evil. The Gothic cathedrals still dotting the European landscape and the numerous artifacts from that period testify to the high regard for craftsmanship, especially in the so-called religious sphere; they also bear witness to the hierarchy controlling medieval society.

One must not idealize the Middle Ages. Those who page the history books in search of the ideal or idyllic society will be as disappointed as those who scan the horizons of the future for a perfect community. This should not prevent us, however, from seeing the positive aspects of the medieval order or from discerning those things that were good and wholesome. One attractive facet of medieval life was the close relationship between land and labour and between master and servant. Land and labour were not commodities for sale on the market. The lords were demanding and their authority was absolute but, in turn, they were obligated to protect and provide for their serfs. Masters in the craft guilds were often autocratic, but the journeyman and the apprentice enjoyed a considerable degree of independence; they commanded respect on the basis of their craftsmanship and guild membership. Further, work was characterized by a leisurely pace and a deep sense of satisfaction. It is interesting to note, for instance, that at the end of the Middle Ages there were no less than 150 statutory holidays, mostly days in honour of saints. France, which retained the medieval patterns of life longer than most European countries, maintained a large number of statutory holidays until the French Revolution in 1789. That explains why the habitants of New France (Quebec) complained to Colbert, Louis XIV's finance minister, that they could not fulfil their task of opening up the new land when, due to the many compulsory holidays, there were only ninety working days left in the year.


## *The Reformation*

The Reformers' rediscovery of the Bible left a deep imprint on the development of the West. The Reformation did not result in an immediate, radical break with the past, as is often assumed. Luther recognized the spiritual equality of all before God, but his railings against the ecclesiastical hierarchy and his exaltation

of peasant life did not prevent him from endorsing a bloody
repression of the peasant revolt, nor did it stop him from
elevating governmental powers in the hands of the nobility. A
monk and peasant himself, Luther was as distrustful of
merchants and bankers as his Catholic opponents were. Calvin,
who had a better understanding than Luther of men's equal
calling as God's stewards in creation, similarly, founded a
regime in Geneva in which christian freedom was at best ill-
understood. One should remember that Luther, Zwingli and
Calvin were children of their age, which was an era of autocracy.
But, while we abhor many of their practices, we must at the
same time recognize the spiritual break they made with the
dualistic character of the Middle Ages. For Luther, all honest
work was honourable and "idleness and covetousness" were sins
which "destroy the unity of the body of which Christians are
members."[3] For Calvin, man's first aim was not personal
salvation but the glorification of God to be sought not by prayer
alone, but also by diligent work. "What reason is there," wrote
Calvin, "why the income from business should not be larger
than that from landowning?"[4] And Zwingli stated: "yet labor is
a thing so good and godlike . . . that [it] makes the body hale
and strong and cures the sicknesses produced by idleness . . . . In
the things of this life, the laborer is most like to God."[5]
The conviction that it is man's duty and privilege to work—
which included business and trade activity—led to an enormous
development in the territories where the Reformation took root.
England and the Low Countries became the new centres of trade
and industry. They were also the countries where freedom began
to flourish and where the first democratic forms of government
found their small beginnings.

## The Renaissance

The Reformation, however, was not the only spiritual
movement which caused the collapse of the medieval order and
influenced the course of events in the sixteenth and seventeenth
centuries. The late Middle Ages witnessed the rebirth and
rediscovery of the arts and philosophies of the Greeks and
Romans. In the ferment of the struggle against the oppressive
shackles of a feudal and ecclesiastical system, a freedom idea

developed which was quite foreign to the Bible. Whereas the
Reformers stressed that man can be free only when he subjects
himself to God and obeys His laws for life, the Renaissance
humanists proclaimed the autonomy of man. Man was said to be
his own lawgiver, in charge of his own destiny. His guiding
light in life was not divine revelation but human reason. Early
scientific discoveries (by Copernicus, Galileo and Da Vinci, for
example) reinforced the conviction that nothing stood in the
way of conquering a hostile nature and that via his own intellect
man would be able to remove the obstacles to a lost paradise.
The humanist concept of man initially remained confined to a
small circle of academics; however, eventually their ideas took
deep roots and were to alter the course of history profoundly.

## The age of Enlightenment

Radical changes in thought and action swept Europe during the
turbulent years of the sixteenth and seventeenth centuries,
ultimately giving rise to what is commonly referred to as the age
of Enlightenment which led to the industrial revolution.

Adam Smith (1723-1790), the world's first great economist,
lived at the very beginning of the industrial revolution. How
vastly different his world was from that of the Reformation two
hundred years earlier or, for that matter, from that of the late
Middle Ages! The medieval doctors of theology exalted spiritual
work, relegated manual labour to a place of secondary
importance, and frowned on all economic motives. Calvin and
Luther restored work to its proper place in creation as a God-
given vocation, but emphasized the need for a God-centred life
of service. Even more than their medieval predecessors, they
condemned the desire to become rich in this world, and they did
not hesitate to condemn and discipline those who pursued
material gain out of economic self-interest.

Not so Adam Smith and his contemporaries. Renaissance
faith in the autonomy of man had rapidly conquered the
lingering medieval patterns of thought in the West. God was no
longer regarded as the living God asking people to serve him
and one another. Instead, God had become some distant being
who, after creating the world, had retired, leaving man the task
to explore and define the laws of nature. In fulfilling this task,

man is not guided by God's revelation, but by reason, that inner light common to all men. This new religion—called deism—is fundamental to Enlightenment developments.

Whereas the medieval fathers and the Reformers taught that we must refrain from merely seeking ourselves, Smith elevated the principle of self-interest to the motivating force in society. "It is not from the benevolence of the butcher, the brewer, or the baker that we expect our dinner," he said, "but from their regard to their own interest. We address ourselves, not to their humanity but to their self-love, and never talk to them of our own necessities but of their advantages."[6] But how is it possible that a society in which everyone is engaged in a mad scramble after self-interest does not fall apart and end up in anarchy? According to Smith, the market prevents this catastrophe. The supposed "invisible hand" of the market will see to it that each gets his due. The laws of the market will show us how self-interest will result in competition, and competition, in turn, will result in the provision of those goods society wants at prices society is prepared to pay. For example, if a glove manufacturer out of self-interest would raise the price of his product above that of his competitors, people automatically would stop buying his gloves. The market would thus force the price down. However, if everyone would want to buy gloves, a shortage of gloves would result, causing the price to rise. Then manufacturers of other products—shoes, for instance—would feel the pinch and would also begin to make gloves. Thus the glove market would soon become saturated, causing an automatic decrease in the price. In turn, this would lead to a decrease in the production of gloves and a greater production of another commodity. In other words, the forces of supply and demand make the market a self-regulating mechanism.

The same law of supply and demand applies, according to Smith, to the population. Workers for him are commodities to be produced in accordance with demand. If wages are high, the number of working people multiplies; if wages fall, this number decreases. In Smith's days infant mortality was shockingly high. "It is not uncommon," says Smith, ". . . in the Highlands of Scotland for a mother who has borne twenty children not to have two alive." Throughout England, half the children lived only to the age of nine or ten. Higher wages, however, will bring about better social conditions resulting in a lower death rate. But then, says Smith, the market mechanism takes over. Heilbroner summarized his arguments as follows: "Just as higher prices on the market will bring about a larger production of gloves and the larger number of gloves in turn press down the higher prices of gloves, so higher wages will bring about a larger number of workers, and the increase in their numbers will set up a reverse pressure on the level of their wages. Population, like glove production, is a self-curing disease—as far as wages are concerned."[7] In the fantasy world of Adam Smith all will be well as long as no one tampers with the market mechanism. Don't try to do good, he says; let good emerge as the byproduct of selfishness.

It is not surprising that the real world showed a different picture. Work was not motivated by a protestant work ethic derived largely from Calvin, as Max Weber asserted in his famous *The Protestant Ethic and the Spirit of Capitalism*. Rather, it was controlled by a humanist work ethic which had its roots in the Renaissance faith that nothing can stop autonomous man from conquering the world by means of his own genius. This work ethic was based on the so-called iron laws of nature; not on God's law of love.

Entrepreneurs adopted the notion developed by John Locke, Adam Smith, David Ricardo, and others, that the real value of every commodity is its labour value. Therefore, the only value of the worker is his capacity to perform work; other than that he has no value. It is important to note here that this idea still prevails strongly in today's labour relations. We will come back to this at a later stage.

Entrepreneurs also readily assented to Smith's dictum that the market—especially the labour market—should be left alone, unhindered by governmental interference.

Smith died in 1790, during the early stages of the industrial revolution, and his lessons had been learned well by the industrialists who changed the face of the earth. As is well known, this was accompanied by the most inhuman situations. Already in Smith's days working conditions were terrible. In the coal mines of Durham and Northumberland men and women worked together, stripped to the waist, under the most inhuman conditions. Children of seven years and older, who never saw daylight during the winter months, slaved away to augment the miners' pitiful wages. Pregnant women drew coal cars like horses and even gave birth in the dark, black caverns of the mines.

After the great inventions of the latter half of the eighteenth century, industrialization accelerated and England became the industrial heartland of the world. The misery which then descended on the workers defies description and is virtually unparalleled in history. Workdays of fourteen and sixteen hours were normal. Little children were carried to the factories by their parents as early as four o'clock in the morning and were often tied to the machines, lest they should fall asleep or run away. They were subjected to brutal treatment by foremen and managers whose authority was unquestioned.

The urge to obtain wealth became the driving force behind the industrial development. The means to that end was work. During the first half of the nineteenth century, the work ethic of incessant hard labour began to assume the nature of a religion. By 1851, the Great Exhibition in the Crystal Palace in London was set up as a showpiece of what work and industry had accomplished. On that occasion *The Economist* printed the following telling editorial:

> Without pretending on the present occasion to appreciate all the bearings of this Exhibition . . . we may briefly notice its moral significance. The Queen of the mightiest empire of the globe—the empire in which industry is the most successfully cultivated, and in which its triumphs have been greatest—was fittingly occupied in consecrating the temple erected to its honour . . . . The contrast and the change we have noticed . . . the former disdain . . . for humble industry, and the present honour it bestows, telling of a future when the hand or the skill of the labourer shall be held in still higher honour . . . —are convincing proofs of the moral improvements already made; and they give us irresistible assurances that a yet higher destiny awaits our successors even on earth.[8]

## The deification of work

It often happens that disciples, thinking they are following in the footsteps of the master, end up saying and doing things which are quite contrary to the master's teachings. This can clearly be seen in the followers of John Calvin.

English and American Puritans, as well as German and Dutch pietists, claiming to be children and heirs of the Reformation, developed a work ethic which deviated sharply from Calvin's ideas. For the Puritans, work, even hard labour, was a divine mandate, whereas leisure was frowned upon as idleness. Success was often seen as a sign of God's favour and the road to success was thrift and hard work. For the Puritans, shalom was not God's free gift which must permeate our entire life. Shalom was reward for diligence. Their interpretation of the fourth commandment placed more emphasis on "six days shalt thou labour" than on "remember the sabbath (rest) day." They observed the letter of the law to the point that the puritan settlers of New England spent most of the Sunday sitting silently at home with blinds drawn to keep the sunlight out.

In eighteenth and nineteenth-century Protestantism there was a strong tendency to identify with the humanist work ethic. John Wesley believed that hard work and a frugal lifestyle were beneficient for the soul. Spurgeon taught that labour was a shield against the temptations of the devil. To prove his point he reminded his audience that in the Bible God appeared to people while they were working: Moses was tending the flock, Gideon was threshing the corn, Elisha was plowing the field, and the disciples were out fishing. (The well-known Dutch theologian and writer Okke Jager makes the ironical remark that Spurgeon conveniently forgot to mention the times God appeared to people in their sleep.)

Did not Calvin teach that to work was to fulfil one's calling and that thrift was to be preferred over extravagance? And did not the new work ethic also urge people to produce for the ultimate good of all? Here, it seems, lies much of the reason why capitalism and Christianity are so often identified and why so many protestant Christians in North America are such ardent supporters of the free-enterprise system.

There is some truth to Max Weber's assertion that the protestant work ethic was linked to Calvinism, although he greatly overstates his case by tracing the argument back to Calvin himself. Calvin's view of labour and leisure was derived more from the promise of shalom God's people may have in Christ. One should note that the Heidelberg Catechism, written by some of Calvin's immediate disciples, explains the fourth commandment in terms of the true sabbath (rest) for all of our lives.

Marxists are also guilty of deviating from their master's teachings. In his early writings, Marx taught that nature will ultimately attain its human destiny and man will reach his natural goal by means of human labour. Only through work does man become fully human. However, Marx also made allowance for man as a multidimensional being whose activities go much beyond hard work. Marx foresaw a society in which the worker could spend much of his time in leisure and would also be able to perform varying tasks.

However, Marx's friend and associate Friedrich Engels, who came from a pietist (puritan) family, and many of his followers, increasingly glorified work as an end in itself. As a result, in marxist countries the worker and his work have taken on a religious significance. Marxists know of only two classes: the working class (proletariat) and the ruling class (bourgeoisie). The former constitutes the elect, the latter the reprobate. Between them runs the line between good and evil. To belong to the working class means sharing in the way of redemption, while to have one's roots in ruling-class circles almost equals being guilty of original sin. Solzhenitsyn, describing the stalinist purges in his *Gulag Archipelago,* states that the interrogators and prosecutors never asked whether the accused was guilty of crimes against socialism, but whether he *could* have been guilty. And the answer to that question depended to a large extent on the defendant's background, i.e., to what class his parents belonged. Solzhenitsyn also states that the authorities in the labour camps of the *Gulag* considered hard work, even inhumanly severe labour, as a *purifying* experience. Such work would have a *cleansing* effect on the polluted mind of the inmate, and would prepare him again for his task in the socialist order. We encounter a similar view in modern China, where the so-called intelligentsia—professors, teachers, nurses and doctors—must spend one year out of every five in communes and factories in order to keep them in touch with the real people, i.e., the workers. It is no coincidence that the hammer and the sickle, symbols of factory and farm, are the regalia of soviet communism.

Nazism, too, overrated and exalted human labour, to the point that Hitler once declared: "Every deed, even a destructive

one, is meaningful; all passivity on the other hand is
meaningless." The slogan "Arbeit macht frei" (Labour makes
free), adorning the entrance gates of the Auschwitz
concentration camp, was not meant to be a macabre joke but
reflected a fundamental belief in the liberating quality of
labour.

Auschwitz represents the supreme irony of the deification of
work.


## *The fall of the idol*


One of the driving forces behind the industrial development
of the nineteenth century was the desire to become wealthy.
Although the desire to gain personal wealth played a large role
(note, for instance, that many entrepreneurs in Europe and
America became immensely rich), the overall goal was to
become wealthy as a nation, for this, in turn, would be to the
benefit of all. This absolutization of wealth and property has
been a characteristic of western civilization over the past 250
years. The dominant motives of our culture no longer consist in
the service of God and neighbour, but in self-fulfilment and the
acquisition of material things.

The desire to accumulate wealth and property had a
demeaning influence on man and thing alike. For it meant that
work, the worker and the product of his hand ultimately became
debased.

To see this more clearly, let us take another look at the era
preceding the Enlightenment. In the medieval order the
craftsman had a certain status. His position was an honourable
one. Although his pay may not have been great, it must be
remembered that high wages were not the goal of life. Society
was static; the aim of life was how to attain the kingdom of
heaven, how to be saved for a life hereafter for which this life was
but a portal. Work was executed in a leisurely manner without
the feverish pace so familiar to us. It was focused on making
products (things) that had meaning transcending earthly life.
Numerous artifacts of those days still exist and they attest to the
fact that a thing was much more than a mere utensil, something
to be used, worn out and discarded. An object was made, used

and handled as having a value that points to God. One sees this probably best expressed in cathedrals and public buildings erected during that period. The same reverence is found in the articles and edifices of the time of the Reformation.

The Enlightenment, with its emphasis on autonomous man, placed man in the centre of life and relegated God and his kingdom to a place of secondary importance. It is not surprising that this shift in the focus of life reflects itself in man's products, in his work, and in his view of the worker. With the advent of mass production, the product became more and more a utensil whose purpose it was to serve man rather than God. Industrial production also diminished the role of craftsmanship; in fact, almost eliminated it. Work itself, from being meaningful, became meaningless—the glowing language of *The Economist* notwithstanding. Thus the product, the work, and the worker were all robbed of their deeper meaning and were subjected to a utilitarian point of view.

It is significant to note in this context how Jeremy Bentham (1748-1832), father of utilitarianism, defined the norm for life when he wrote: "Nature has placed mankind under the governance of two sovereign masters, *pain* and *pleasure*. It is for them alone to point out what we ought to do, as well as to determine what we shall do. On the one hand the standard of right and wrong, on the other the chain of causes and effects, are fastened to their throne. They [pain and pleasure] govern us in all we do, in all we say, in all we think; every effort we can make to throw off our subjection will serve but to demonstrate and confirm it." "Pleasure," says Bentham, "is the only good . . . and pain is the only evil."[9] These, in other words, are the new norms for all of human behaviour, and they replace the biblical norms for good and evil, right and wrong. Economists and industrialists alike adopted Bentham's dictum and began to consider the possession of consumption goods as a pleasure (hence good) and the performance of work as a pain (hence evil). Obviously, this notion is diametrically opposed to what the Bible teaches about these matters. It frequently warns against the possession of many material things, and it upholds work as inherently human and part of God's mandate for man.

From being deified, work as such now became a pain and fell from its newly gained pedestal of worship.

# Technology—a Frankenstein

This presented a new problem. For how could the goals of maximum production of goods with the smallest amount of labour be accomplished? Here technology began to play its crucial role in the industrial development of the West. Increasingly the machine took over the work of man. An endless series of technical inventions, together with the discovery of seemingly inexhaustible energy resources (initially coal; later oil and gas) radically changed the process of production. Technology was the key to the solution of this new problem.

One often hears the complaint that the machine has enslaved man. To some extent this is true, provided we remember that man first enslaved himself to ideas that did not spring from God's revelation and his norms for human life but arose from an apostate heart. The machine has indeed become a Frankenstein monster, a creation of man which now seems to exert a tyrannical influence over him. For technology not only dictates what the worker shall make and how he shall make it; it also eliminates the worker himself from the production process. Not the labourer, nor the production method or the product, but production itself has become the primary goal of industry. Let's take a closer look at what happened to the role of the worker, the production method, and the product.

## 1. *The worker.*

Unlike his predecessor, the worker of the nineteenth and twentieth centuries has been degraded to a mere production factor. The heartrending conditions prevailing in the mines and factories of Europe and America during the previous century have already been mentioned. Men, women and children worked long hours per day for starvation wages. They were considered less important than tools and machinery. (It is the tragedy of the trade-union movement to this day that it has frequently not understood the fundamental problem of the worker, i.e., his degradation to a cost factor.) Today this view of the worker is still as prevalent as it was 150 years ago. An employee is not employed because he is a creature of God, called to use his talents in his work. In fact, the worker himself is not employed at all. He is hired *only* for his capacity to contribute to production, for which he is paid a certain fee. His being hired and fired is dictated by the demand of the production process; he is only paid for the minutes and hours he contributes to production. No less and no more. The employer does not believe he has any further obligation to his workers. Or, to put it in the words of Milton Friedman, one of America's most influential economists and recent Nobel laureate:

> Few trends could so thoroughly undermine the very foundations of our free society as the acceptance by corporate officials of a social responsibility other than to make as much money for their stockholders as possible. This is a fundamentally subversive doctrine.[10]

Friedman's callousness is not restricted to an academic issue. The utterly cynical attitude which trade unions encounter on the part of many employers testifies to the fact that there is no real appreciation for the worker. High wages are paid only because of trade union pressure or because they are an incentive to higher productivity, or both. At bottom we are dealing here with a view of the enterprise which is contrary to the biblical concept of stewardship. The enterprise is regarded as an object of absolute ownership by shareholders, and the purpose of the enterprise is to generate a maximum return on investments. Within this conception there is no room for the idea that the enterprise is a work community in which differently talented people (managers, engineers, salesmen, office staff, and blue-collar workers) have their own rightful place and task as full-fledged associates.

## 2. *The production method.*

The degradation of the worker and the drive for greater productivity resulted in a working milieu and production methods that were inhuman. In the eighteenth century, hundreds of thousands of peasants in Europe, especially in England, were forced off the land by the Enclosure movement and were put to work in factory caverns to perform mind-numbing tasks under despotic supervision. The industrial work methods left these former farmers no opportunity to use their own initiative or even to enjoy the sunlight. As the years went by, mechanization and regimentation greatly increased on the

assumption that these would raise efficiency. In America,
Frederick Taylor went so far as to develop certain scientific-
management methods by measuring in number of seconds the
time needed for each movement of the arm, the leg, and the
body. The worker was to operate in rigidly and minutely
prescribed manners to ensure minimal waste of time and
maximal productivity. Subsequently, Taylorism was
introduced in industries throughout the western world, and
even today the industrial engineer with his stopwatch is a
familiar sight in most of our plants. The monotony of work
itself, together with lack of even physical freedom, has stifled
workers' initiative, causing tensions and industrial unrest
which are expressed in frequent strikes and even in sabotage.
Work that is considered to be a disutility (a pain) almost
inevitably turns out to be just that.


### 3. *The product.*

Our consumption and production-oriented lifestyle not only
debases the worker and his work, but also debauches the fruit of
his labour, i.e., the product. It is frequently said that, due to
the endless division of tasks, an assembly-line worker cannot
point to the end product with any degree of pride and say "this is
what I have made." However, there is another important reason
why he cannot do so, for there is nothing to be proud of.
Products have become cheap, not only with respect to price, but
especially with respect to quality. The product has, for the most
part, lost its intrinsic value as an object that expresses man's
creativity and devotion to God. Instead, it has become a
disposable item to be used and discarded.

Our industrial system aims at the rapid production and
consumption of more and more goods. Current Timex
commercials, for example attempt to convince us that we must
wear a different watch to each different occasion, such as work,
church, shopping, the tennis court, and a party. The life of a
product is deliberately shortened to ensure continuous
production. Fashions, similarly (whether pertaining to
refrigerators or clothes), are intentionally altered to make room
for newer products.

Moreover, the market is flooded with items that should not
be made at all. These range from artificial fingernails to rose-

scented toiletpaper. In this connection Galbraith keenly observes that we can choose between ten different underarm sprays (for our protection) while much-needed social workers are often not available.

When the purpose of life becomes the accumulation of wealth and the consumption of things, society is degraded to a collection of consumers. Furthermore, when work becomes a disutility, necessary but undesirable, the total effect becomes a movement toward increased mechanization and automation which eliminates the worker and creates stubborn structural unemployment. After all, if energy and the machine can replace human work and still ensure a steady stream of products, then let's convert to automation. The gradual takeover of human labour by the machine is evident from statistical trends. In 1850, seventy percent of America's population was employed in agriculture; today this figure stands at five percent. Where did all these farmers and farm workers go? They were replaced by the machine and began to drift to the cities to find work in the growing industrial apparatus. At the turn of the century we find about sixty percent of American wage earners employed in industry. They did not stay there, however. Today, industrial workers constitute only twenty-three percent of the workforce. In other words, the shift persisted; workers continued to be replaced by the machine. But where did they go this time? Again, statistics supply the answer. Currently, fifty to fifty-five percent of the workforce is employed in the so-called service sector of society instead of the agricultural or industrial sector. The service sector includes hydro repairmen, teachers, policemen, nurses, civil servants and salesmen. This enormous change came about especially since the end of the second world war, when a revolutionary process in automation soon eliminated millions of industrial jobs. *The Economist* of December 25, 1976, predicts that this shift will continue and that during the lifetime of most people alive today the present percentage (23%) of industrial workers in the workforce will drop to five percent. For many years it was thought that the service sector, together with leisure activity, would largely replace industrial work. Hence the influx of students to colleges and universities during the past decade, to the extent that these institutions could hardly cope with it. We have found out the hard way that the number of available jobs as teachers, professors, nurses, and civil servants is also limited, as a consequence of which countless graduates are now unemployed or underemployed.

The prostitution of the product, the debasement of work, and the gradual elimination of the worker have been accompanied by a steady increase in production and productivity. Our gross national product—that magic figure which expresses the dollar value of the total annual output of final goods and services in a nation—continues to grow and is regarded as the barometer of our national well-being. For many years it was thought that our economy would and could grow indefinitely. Our highly automated industry would see to it that our enormous appetite for more consumer goods would be amply satisfied.

This golden dream has now abruptly ended and is slowly turning into a nightmare. Although some heard the rumblings of the gathering storm much earlier, the severe energy crisis of 1973 and the rather sudden realization that our environment can only bear so much, caused economic shockwaves that were felt everywhere. It is finally realized that the earth's resources and the environment's resilience are not infinite but finite. Instead of expectations of unlimited growth, we are now faced with severe strictures. The tripling of energy costs, the expense of pollution control, the unwillingness of corporations to reduce profits and lower prices, and the reluctance of trade unions to lessen their wage demands, are main factors in the inflation that threatens the foundations of the industrialized world. The resultant deceleration of production (about twenty percent of our productive machinery is idle or under-utilized) has led to unusually high unemployment levels which in several European countries even exceed those of the depression of the thirties.

Finally, at present we also witness the uncommon phenomenon of simultaneous inflation and unemployment. If nothing else has done so, this has shattered our optimistic belief that the economy is immune to crises.


## Why work anyway?

At this rather dismal juncture, what prospects are there for renewal and restoration of work? Before I outline some concrete proposals, we must take a look at the nature of work itself. Work is a typical *human* activity. Animals do not work because they carry no responsibility. It is for this reason that animals never get bored even though they perform the same task over and over again. Man's task, however, needs to be performed responsibly because every facet ultimately derives from a single divine mandate. In other words, in his work man *responds* to, gives an *answer* to God who calls him to service, for work is a calling. Naturally, we should say more, but this embodies the basic answer to the question: "Why work anyway?"

In history we see that God blesses man when he performs his task in obedience to the divine norms of stewardship. The faithful servant, who will be busy when the Master comes, shall be rewarded in the present as well as in the hereafter. Despite the curse of sin, man may enjoy the fruits of his labours and may rejoice in the product of his hands, because his handiwork mirrors God's handiwork. Man is not doomed to slavish labour all the days of his life. The satisfaction derived from his daily work and the joyful reflection on his accomplishments presuppose the enjoyment of leisure and rest.

Work has four foci, each distinct, yet inseparable. First of all, work is a form of *worship* in which God the Creator and Redeemer is at the centre. This may seem incongruous to our modern society; yet God demands our wholehearted service and devotion in every aspect of our existence, including those pertaining to our daily work. The object of our work-worship should be God; not the product we make. Even the most durable of our products will eventually decay or be destroyed; yet, if made in devotion to God, they will in a sense endure forever. We are assured of this in Revelation 14:13 where we read: "'Blessed are the dead who die in the Lord henceforth.' 'Blessed indeed,' says the Spirit, 'that they may rest from their labors, for their deeds follow them!'" (R.S.V.)

The fruits of our labour and the product of our hands must point to Him who calls us to his service. This applies as much to the social worker who serves a neighbour in need as it does to a construction worker who lays bricks or hangs doors. Our work must indeed be dedicated to the Lord. Worship of God cannot be confined to prayer, preaching or hymnsinging. A truly religious understanding of work implies the recognition that it is man's particular mission on earth, his response to God's call. Man is responsible to God in all things; in *whether* he works, in *how* he works, and *to what purpose* he works.

In the second place, work is meant to *ennoble* mankind. Work should provide us with a profound sense of satisfaction; it should give us a sense of self-fulfilment. For a factory not only shapes products, it also shapes people. A nurse not only helps the patient, she also helps herself. It is, therefore, deeply tragic that countless workers in our society are deprived of the satisfaction of accomplishment due to the nature and structure of their work. Such people are virtually forced to seek happiness in leisure and the possession of goods.

Work also entitles us to rewards or wages, which enable us to provide for ourselves, our family, and our neighbour. Moreover, as imagebearers of God, we should and may express ourselves in our work. Man can perpetuate himself in the fruits of his labour; from the product of his hands it should be evident to him that it is what *he* has made rather than someone else.

Thirdly, work is directed to one's *neighbour*. It must indeed be both "good" and a "service." Society must truly benefit from our work. This biblical notion was clearly set forth by John Calvin in his *Institutes* in which he explained that God did not create people differently to accentuate inequality, but to stimulate their interdependence. Precisely because they have different gifts and talents, men and women must help and support one another.

Finally, our place and task as stewards in God's estate requires *stewardly care* over all of creation, including the earth's potentialities and resources. As stewards we own nothing, since the earth has been given to us in trust. We must manage God's property in such a manner that his name is honoured and our neighbour's well-being is genuinely served. Obviously, we cannot continue to squander the wealth of nations, such as oil and gas, gold and steel, thereby leaving our neighbour at home or abroad without the necessities for life. Nor may we endanger life on this planet by destroying the air and the oceans. We must preserve and protect to the best of our abilities.

# The road of renewal

As we noted earlier, the sudden realization that the earth and its resources are finite and that human happiness cannot be equated with unlimited possession of goods, has severely jarred our society and has placed man before a choice. Either we continue on the same road which leads to ultimate destruction, or we begin to look for alternatives. The Berger Report, perhaps more than anything else, has confronted us with that choice. Similarly, the dead-end street of collective bargaining has caused governments to reflect on our dismal record and to explore new ways of structuring the work situation.

It is clear that we must travel a different route. It is also clear that going that route involves enormous difficulties, for it requires more than a grudging recognition of the facts of life. It means a conscious repudiation of the gods of technology, growth, and progress. However, the very fact that these gods are forsaking us today opens up opportunities to gain new insights and to direct our attention to the God of heaven and earth who, like the father in the story of the prodigal son, is waiting for our return. What is at stake here is the total redirection of our society. It does not help to rely on noneffective, instant solutions.

The late, well-known English economist E.F. Schumacher, in his bestseller *Small is Beautiful,* made an eloquent plea for the introduction of intermediate technology, i.e., a much simpler technology which utilizes more human labour and less energy. He advocated this kind of technology especially for the third world, but there is no reason why it could not be used extensively in the West as well. Our dwindling, ever-more-expensive energy resources, together with our structural unemployment, cry out for more labour-intensive industry. Technology has become a curse since it enslaves the worker and makes him superfluous—all because we placed our ultimate hope and happiness in the machine. However, it can become a blessing if it is used to enrich our work. Therefore, a turn to more labour-intensive, energy-saving technology will not only help us solve problems of energy shortage, structural unemployment, and even inflation, but can also make work itself more meaningful. To be sure, certain fields, such as medicine, mining, aircraft industry, defence, and the development and application of solar energy, will continue to require highly complex technology. But a large number of the products necessary for our life can be simplified as well as produced in a much simpler manner than is the case today.

In an article published in *The Catholic Worker* of February 1977, Schumacher wrote:

> People say it can't be done; small scale is uneconomic. How do they know? While the idea that "bigger is better" may have been a 19th century truth, now, owing to the advance of knowledge and technical ability, it has become—not all along the line, but over wide fields of application—a twentieth century myth.
>
> I have in mind, as an example, a production unit developed by the Intermediate Technology Development Group which costs around $5000. The smallest unit previously available cost $250,000, fifty times as much, and had a capacity about 50 times as great. The makers of this large-scale unit were completely convinced that any smaller unit would be hopelessly uneconomic. But they were wrong. Think of it: instead of one unit requiring for its efficient operation a vast and complicated organization, we can now have fifty units, each of them "on the human scale," each of them large enough for a few enterprising people to make an honest living, but none of them so large as to make anyone inordinately rich. Think of the simplification of transport if there can be many small units instead of one large one, each of them drawing on local raw materials and working for nearby local markets. Think of the social and individual human consequences of such a change of scale.[11]

One area of manufacturing where the need for less capital-intensive and more labour-intensive industry is most obvious and acute is the petrochemical field. Since the end of the second world war the petrochemical industry has undergone a meteoric development. Countless products, formerly made of leather, linen, cotton, wool, rubber, wood, and steel, are now being made from synthetic materials such as plastics, detergents, and synthetic fibres. This industry, moreover, has a built-in tendency to proliferate, since the processes involved generate a large amount of waste which, in turn, almost invariably is converted into a large number of byproducts. That development

has at least three serious consequences. In the first place, it has
become increasingly evident that many petrochemical products
are carcinogens and are considered to be the main cause of the
alarming increase in cancer. Especially for this reason, PCB, DDT,
and other chlorinated hydrocarbon insecticides had to be
banned from the market. Secondly, as we all know, the
petrochemical industry depends heavily on an abundant supply
of crude oil and gas, since its products are extracted from these
fuels. However, during the past five years we have become
painfully aware of the limitations of such a supply. Our
indiscriminate use of the earth's resources now boomerangs on
us in that it threatens society with a depletion of the traditional
energy resources within the next two generations. Thirdly, the
petrochemical industry is extremely capital-intensive; it
employs a comparatively small number of workers and causes
severe unemployment in those industries which still
manufacture products from traditional materials. Only large-
scale enterprises in the petrochemical field can remain
competitive because the extremely costly installations and
equipment which are required are prohibitive to industries with
limited markets. In other words, the petrochemical industry
not only devours a large slice of our dwindling energy resources;
it also places a very heavy demand on the scarce supply of
available capital.

Today, many knowledgeable observers advocate a large-scale
return to less costly, more labour-intensive manufacture which
employs traditional materials, such as leather, linen, wool,
soap, etc.[12]


It is obvious that a mere shift from complex to intermediate
technology and the alleviation of unemployment will not
restore the worker, his work, and the product to their respective
honourable positions.

The unemployed are not the only ones who experience a sense
of uselessness and futility. Many of those still at work are just as
frustrated because their jobs do not leave room for any freedom
and initiative. Monotony is not always the sole culprit of
frustration. But monotony, combined with rigidly enforced
discipline, the stifling of initiative, and the production of
useless or inferior products, makes work a drudgery to be

endured rather than to be enjoyed. The current industrial
system of tight control over the worker and his work must be
replaced by work communities in which the worker actively
participates. This requires a substantial degree of workers'
codetermination in the decision making that goes on every day
on the shopfloor. It is important to note here that I am not
advocating the abolition of authority. Authority is a
prerequisite for the proper functioning of the enterprise. The
marxist option of workers' control is based on a blind ideology
rather than on the scriptural norms for authority. To bear
authority and provide leadership requires peculiar talents which
many people do not possess. But the true mark of authority is
that it fosters freedom and responsibility. Workers who sense
and experience that their presence on the shopfloor, in the
office, or on the jobsite is only required because of their capacity
to increase production and profits, will nearly always be
resentful and rebellious, no matter how high their pay may be.
In contrast, workers who are treated as associates in a work
community where there is respect, appreciation, and a sense of
contribution to the needs of society, will enjoy their work even
when the pay is relatively low.

In this context the Christian Labour Association of Canada
has urged the federal and provincial governments to enact
legislation which makes it mandatory for enterprises with one
hundred or more employees to establish enterprise councils in
which workers' representatives and managers jointly discuss and
decide policies that pertain to everyday work. The CLAC has also
advocated a form of codetermination which grants workers
equal representation with shareholders on the boards of
directors of such firms. Major decisions concerning the future of
the enterprise as a work community cannot be left to those who
only have a financial interest in the company. It is not expected
that legislation will bring about a change in mentality. But
proper legislation does influence the thinking and attitudes of
all and can be a powerful incentive for fairer relationships on the
job.

As to the product, I believe that a combined effort to provide
meaningful work and establish equitable working conditions
will greatly contribute to a qualitative improvement of the
product.

# Conclusion

Where does this leave you and me? It leaves us in the position
where Christians should always be; namely, in the witness box.
We must first of all reveal something of Christ's liberation in
our personal and communal lifestyle. This does not mean that
we should be puritan killjoys whose rule of life is: "don't taste,
don't touch, don't handle." But it does mean that we should
resist the temptations of doing all the things the Joneses do.
Further, we should develop a keen sensitivity to our own
consumption habits and to the needs of others. We should
question such things as whether we really need bathrooms full of
cosmetics (for our protection), a colour TV, the latest car, a
bigger house, the endless stream of gadgets that enchant for a
while and then are thrown into the garbage. We might also
reexamine the luxury of making an annual pilgrimage to
Jamaica, Barbados or Acapulco. I am not suggesting that we
should never take our vacation there, but I am questioning the
wisdom of regularly displaying our riches to poverty-stricken
nations and I wonder what influence such vacations have on
schoolchildren who yearly observe the absence of a number of
fellow students during the winter months.

It may well be that a more sober and responsible individual
lifestyle has little impact on society as a whole—though such
impact is often underestimated. But our personal relationship
to God should always come first—and can we face him when our
private manner of life is characterized by extravagance and
waste?

However, a christian witness which addresses itself to a
redirection of society may never be restricted to personal
testimonies and individual lifestyles. It is lamentable that
North American evangelicals, on the whole, have not
understood this. By reducing the Bible to a collection of moral
presuppositions and prescriptions, evangelicalism has failed to
grasp the normative character of God's revelation for social,
economic, and political life. As a result, neither the
ramifications of sin, nor the scope of Christ's redemption, were
fully understood, and the christian life was largely confined to
individual, moral behaviour.

The Word of God is not a code of ethics or a manual for

correct *savoir faire*. It is the living and life-giving Word in which God calls man to an obedient response in every dimension of his life. That constitutes the essence of human responsibility. Wherever human structures—whether they be corporations, trade unions or political movements—obstruct rather than promote the exercise of that responsibility, Christians must ensure that their oneness in the Spirit visibly expresses itself. Thus the primary task of a christian trade union is to manifest this unity and to offer alternatives which allow all workers the freedom and the opportunity to use their talents and responsibilities in the service of God and fellowmen.

To be sure, establishing christian trade unions, schools, and political movements is not without risk. History is replete with examples of organizations and institutions which claimed to be christian but, in fact, were not. Even today there are many groups for whom the word *christian* (sometimes unwittingly) serves as a masquerade for an ideology, such as apartheid, marxism or free enterprise. Such groups greatly discredit the name of Christ and help nullify the effect of genuinely christian communal witness. Here we are reminded of the words of the apostle Paul: "Let every one who names the name of the Lord depart from iniquity." (II Timothy 2:19;R.S.V.)

But even those who are aware of ideological snares must constantly be on the alert to discern the spirits at work in the world—a task which is easily underestimated. It requires much prayer, a deep sense of dependence on God's Spirit, a healthy dose of humility (for we know only in part) and a willingness to constantly reexamine one's position in the many complexities that face us. However, it requires an equally bold determination to forge ahead in the unshakable conviction that our obedient adherence to the Word of God will yield unprecedented fruits. For that Word is crystal clear with respect to the purpose and destiny of man in God's world, which includes the world of work. Rather than stay aloof and criticize from a distance, Christ-confessors should band together and support those associations which clearly demonstrate their openness to God's call for obedience.

To accomplish a redirection of our culture is no easy task. We must bear in mind, however, that at the centre of all our efforts is the church. It is here that the new consorting in

Jesus Christ should become most manifest, for it is here that our faith is most openly confessed. The church is not an institution whose task it is to speak authoritatively on all kinds of detailed issues. It should be very hesitant, for instance, to endorse the platform of a political party or trade union, even when such organizations profess to be christian. Not only does the church in general lack the insight and expertise to judge complex social, economic, and political matters; pronouncements on issues in those areas of life could easily conflict with the peculiar nature and task of the church. The church is an institution of *all* Christ-believers and its calling is to proclaim the Word of God. This Word gives no detailed prescriptions for each and every situation confronting us. It does, however, give a clear Direction for life and that Direction must reveal itself in the life of the church itself as well as its members.

The church should, therefore, rejoice whenever its members establish and support institutions and organizations of a genuinely christian nature, for this is an indication that the Word of God has fallen in fertile soil and has begun to bear fruit. When his happens, we can together pray the prayer of Moses, the man of God:

> Let thy work be manifest to thy servants,
> and thy glorious power to their children.
> Let the favor of the Lord our God be upon us,
> and establish thou the work of our hands upon us,
> yea, the work of our hands establish thou it.
> (Psalm 90: 16, 17; R.S.V.)

### Notes

1. Cf. Robert L. Heilbroner, *The Economic Problem* (Englewood Cliffs, N.J.: Prentice-Hall, 1968), p. 32.

2. *Ibid.*

3. Cf. R. H. Tawney, *Religion and the Rise of Capitalism* (New York: Harcourt, Brace & Co., 1926; reprint ed., New York: The New American Library, A Mentor Book, 1947), p. 83.

4. *Ibid.*, p. 93.

5. *Ibid.*, p. 101.

6. Adam Smith, *The Wealth of Nations* (1776; New York: The Modern Library, 1937), p. 14.

7. Cf. Robert L. Heilbroner, *The Worldly Philosophers* (New York: Simon and Schuster, 1953), pp. 59 and 59, 60 resp.

8. *The Economist,* vol. IX, no. 401 (May 3, 1851), p. 474.

9. Jeremy Bentham, *The Principles of Morals and Legislation* (New York: Hafner, 1949), pp. 1 and 2 respectively.

10. Milton Friedman, *Capitalism and Freedom* (Chicago: The University of Chicago Press, 1962), p. 133.

11. E. F. Schumacher, "Philosophy of Work," *The Catholic Worker*, vol. XLIII, no. 2 (February 1977), p. 8.

12. Cf., for instance, Barry Commoner's well-documented plea for such a turn-about in "The Promise and Perils of Petrochemicals," *The New York Times Magazine,* 25 September 1977, pp. 38ff.

# 3
# Socioethical Aspects of Labour <sup>*</sup>

*by* Peter Nijkamp

Present-day labour problems receive increasing attention and are a substantial ingredient of our daily news. There is, however, no concensus about the roots of nor the remedies for these problems. On the contrary, different views of labour seem to cleave western societies.

## Different views of labour

Some people look upon recent high unemployment rates as symptoms of a coming crisis which will be even more serious than the depression of the thirties. In their opinion, a catastrophe such as an "ecospasm" (Toffler) is imminent, because western societies are reaching the borders of their capacities, while science and technology are unable to repel current and future threats.

---

*   *Lecture presented at the Institute for Christian Studies, Toronto, June 2, 1977. In part it is based on Peter Nijkamp and N. Vogelaar,* Verlegenheid rond werkgelegenheid [*Embarrassment Concerning Employment*] (*Groningen, The Netherlands: De Vuurbaak, 1977*).

According to others, current unemployment rates are signs of a new state in social history, characterized by leisure, when man will be freed from the oppressive burdens of an achievement society and of the cares for his daily bread.

These very different views of labour have deeper sociocultural and socioethical roots. The first view reflects the conviction that to a certain extent man in his work (the so-called *homo faber*) may transcend nature, but that nature imposes clear restraints on man's activities so that, despite human efforts, a realm of unlimited possibilities (utopia) will never be attained. Social, economic, and cultural history reflects the tragedy of human activities.

The second view expresses optimism in human history. History is progress! Human labour is a necessary tool to arrive at a future state where the fetters of nature detaining man are shattered. Labour and culture raise man above plants and animals. Today's problems are prerequisites for attaining a future leisure state. In other words, it is necessary as it were to climb over a ridge before getting to a fertile valley!

These divergent views illustrate that work can be judged in different and even opposite ways; *homo faber* can be conceived of either as a creator of culture or as a prisoner of nature. These ideas also illustrate that labour constitutes the pivot of our society. Conceptions of labour have a central place in social and cultural philosophy as well as in present-day politics. Serious and deep reflection on the meaning of work is necessary before we can make a single significant statement about such current problems as the growth/steady-state dilemma, depletion of resources, environmental deterioration, intermediate technology, and third-world issues.

Labour ethics also plays a central role in the calvinist view of the world, which stresses the biblical task of man—that he should manage and unfold the earth in order to honour his Creator, to serve his fellowmen, and to develop society in a responsible manner. The christian conception of labour rightly plays a crucial role in christian social, economic, and political thinking.

A closer analysis of the history of economic thought during the last centuries demonstrates that, in general, views of labour take a central place in economic debates.

# *Labour in the history of economic of thought*

The history of economic thought demonstrates many oscillations, many ups and downs, just like the economic process itself. A wide variety of socioeconomic philosophies and schools have succeeded each other. Each stage in this history appeared to have its own specific character, an interest in its own specific problems.

It is striking, however, that, in spite of substantial discrepancies in scientific approaches to socioeconomic problems, one subject almost always received central attention; namely, the question of the *place, function, and significance of labour*. The concept of labour and its meaning in societal processes has been of major importance in economic reflection. I hope to briefly illustrate this by means of several examples from the development of economic thought during the last centuries.

The *mercantilist* period (end seventeenth century) was marked by the economic notion that a nation's wealth consisted primarily in a limited quantity of gold and silver. Apart from extraction, the best manner to obtain gold and silver was via forceful promotion of international trade. Increasing export, however, requires competitive prices and these, in turn, require low wage costs. Consequently, the mercantilist view of the world with its emphasis on wealth necessitated the existence and promotion of a large number of hard-working but poor labourers with low incomes. The *homo faber* was a mere derivative of the struggle for increased national power. Mercantilist labour ethics implied essentially the absence of any labour ethics. Man himself was not that important; only the product of his hands counted.

During the *physiocratic* period (mid-eighteenth century) much stress was placed on agriculture. Mother earth was the only source of a net production value. Agricultural employment was especially important because it gave rise to a net production increase. Employment in other sectors was considered to be less meaningful, for wealth and income as such were regarded as sterile. Only living nature could provide growth. Physiocratic ethics was essentially based on a "return to nature," in contrast to mercantilism with its depreciation of the agricultural labour force. In the physiocratic view of the world, only agriculturally productive labour counted as a way to increase wealth.

The *classical* economists (end eighteenth and early nineteenth centuries) placed human labour in the centre of their analysis because labour, in their opinion, was the source of all wealth. Division of labour was important because this would lead to increased productivity. Further, each member of society had a natural right to labour. Division of labour among different social classes in society was supposed to take place by means of what Adam Smith called the "invisible hand" which guaranteed that every individual would attain his rightful place so that natural harmony would be achieved. These ideas of labour and its division formed the basis for economic liberalism. The classical view of the world with its emphasis on division of labour by an "invisible hand" as constituting the basis of national wealth certainly meant that the jobs of all individuals counted.

*Marxism* also focuses much attention on the place of labour in society. Here also labour determines wealth and welfare. But the main difference with the classical view is that, according to marxism, individuals do not live in natural harmony with one another. On the contrary, there are two classes: a ruling class and an oppressed class; these live in continual mutual struggle without any chance of reconciliation. Marxists believe that class struggle is a fundamental feature of past socioeconomic developments. Thus capitalists exploited proletarians because human labour was undervalued. And alienation is a great evil which should be combated with all means in order to restore harmony between man and his work. The ethics of labour is the heart of marxism. Labour counts!

In the *neoclassical* view (beginning of the twentieth century) much attention was paid to individual utility or welfare accruing from production and employment. Neoclassical economics advocated the maximization of personal utility on which basis labour should be employed in the production process. Free competition was generally assumed to provide maximum social—i.e., the aggregate of individual—utility so that here again an economic basis for liberalism was provided. In the neoclassical view, labour had primarily a derivative value; it served to satisfy individual wants and welfare. It should be added, however, that, especially after the crisis of the thirties, problems of employment also began to play an important role, particularly in the keynesian version of this view of economics.

*Postwar* economic thinking placed much emphasis on both a socially desirable distribution of incomes among all individuals and a macroeconomic equilibrium with full employment. Not so much a maximization of individually perceived utility but rather a general maximization of income and production became paramount. Postwar growth ideology in practice led to a subordinate position of labour in that it derived its meaning mainly from its contribution to welfare. Quality of labour was frequently neglected.

Increased production was judged necessary to achieve economic and social progress and to channel existing discontent. Continuous economic growth was considered effective medicine for structural economic ills like unemployment and unequal distribution. This expansion ideology has caused many severe problems during the last decade, such as environmental decay and exhaustion of resources. Economic growth has exceeded the limits of our society as far as its physical, environmental, and spiritual resources are concerned. As a result of the stress on macroeconomic equilibrium in the market, the qualitative aspects of labour in a microeconomic sense (such as individual labour satisfaction) were largely neglected. This point will be discussed in greater detail below.

In summary, various views of labour have played a decisive and directive role in the history of economic thought and in the socioeconomic development of the last few hundred years. Therefore, reason exists to dwell somewhat longer on the meaning and function of human labour. As a beginning to such reflection, some attention must be paid to the rise of organized trade unions in western societies, to demonstrate the close link between conceptions of labour and sociopolitical labour organizations.


## Labour and unions

Labour and unions appear to be inseparable today. Unionization can be explained from various historical circumstances. First, the miserable conditions of many labourers during the previous century must be mentioned. To a certain extent, the sociopolitical organization of labourers can be seen as a reaction to degrading work and living conditions, though it should be added that in earlier centuries also economic conditions were far from favourable. Another reason for the rise of unions in several countries consisted in the self-interest of more highly paid labourers in order to maintain their economic power position via institutionalized organizations. (An important impetus for labour organization in the Netherlands was given by diamond workers, for instance.) Furthermore, a certain idealism on the part of the cultural elite also played a significant role in the development of labour unions.

An important economic condition favouring the rise of labour unions was the geographic concentration of labourers as a result of the industrial revolution. The so-called factory proletariat was able to organize itself in unions both because of its size and its concentration. The unskilled labour class, which only had hands to work with, felt so exploited and humiliated by the factory owners that a tight mass organization was judged to be the only means to constitute a countervailing power. According to marxism, the owners were not interested in the meaningfulness of labour, but only in the commodities produced by it.

It is not hard to understand why marxist ideas, especially about class struggle and exploitation of labour, found easy acceptance among the working class, particularly in those areas where liberalism was dominant or where the church neglected social abuse and social disaster.

It should be emphasized, however, that the church itself in general cannot be accused of neglect of social problems. The church has indeed failed in several respects, but there also are many examples from the history of evangelical churches which demonstrate that the church took its diaconal task seriously under difficult socioeconomic circumstances.

In summary, all social conditions of the nineteenth century played a role in the rise of labour unions. Unfortunately, the main roots of unionization spring from marxist views of labour and labour conditions. The widespread influence of marxist ideas is in my opinion the result of two forces: the militancy and aggressiveness of marxist doctrine with respect to justice and exploitation, and the marxist proclamation of a new future society.

For example, in *Communist Manifesto* (1848) Marx stated that the ruling class (bourgeoisie) no longer is capable of executing its task because its actions and decisions lead to an ever-increasing humiliation and alienation of the working class. Therefore, the historical task of the proletariat is to perform a world-liberating act, so that the ruling class will be shaken by a communist revolution. The proletariat has nothing to lose but its chains and it has a world to gain. The threatening and militant call to the proletariat of all countries to join forces indicates clearly that marxist thinking is not abstract, but a concrete political design for society of an ideological and antichristian nature. Religion is even labeled the opiate of a nation because it offers people hope of future salvation while neglecting current misery.

It is obvious that marxism is directly concerned with human labour. Labour distinguishes man from animals. Human history is the history of productive forces and labour conditions. Labour is the key to becoming a real man. The reason why marxism protests against dehumanized labour in a capitalist production system is that in such a system man offers his labour as merchandise, so that a capitalist earns money from the supply of labour and the labourer becomes alienated from himself. In that situation labour does not imply a realm of free development but of social detention. The capitalist himself is not guilty of this situation; he is merely the victim of a socioeconomic system based on a private-enterprise economy and on free competition. Therefore, in marxist opinion, a prerequisite to combat exploitation and alienation is collective and common ownership of the former private means of production.

In a period of great political instability and socioeconomic misery the convincing power of marxism seduced thousands of people to support the ideas of class struggle and social self-salvation. Even among Christians a number of people were attracted to marxist doctrine. Fortunately, many Christians warned against the misleading ideas of this doctrine and even started their own organizations based on a concept of harmony between employers and employees. A good example is the Dutch alliance called *Patrimonium,* which made a serious attempt to reject the idea of class struggle and to create a socioeconomic institutional structure based on a joint task for all social classes.

Unfortunately, the notion of conflicting classes has received much support from socialist and communist, as well as from christian side. Divergent views of labour and its use in western economic systems appear to have caused a break in society which is unequaled in the socioeconomic history of the last few centuries. The idea of conflict appears to be opposed to the idea of harmony and cooperation between social partners. This fundamental difference has had enormous consequences. First, internationally two enormous power blocs came about: East versus West. But also in the West itself a profound rupture took place because political parties and labour unions took the social-conflict model as their ideological starting point. The socio-economic and political climate of many western countries is primarily determined by a sociopolitical quest for emancipation in every area. Questions regarding the fundamental value of labour and a just labour division and income appear to have split up our society both socially and politically. The social-conflict view of labour has led to major repercussions for our socioeconomic institutional organization.

This complaint about the conflict pattern which controls much of western society certainly does not mean a plea for a capitalist socioeconomic system. On the contrary, the capitalist system suffers from the same failures as the marxist one. Free competition among entrepreneurs also leads to a life-and-death struggle with serious repercussions for employment, nature, and the third world. Expansion ideology, the engine of a capitalist system, fosters a materialist disposition in which love for material things overshadows love for God and neighbour. Therefore, no reason exists to support capitalism as an alternative to marxism, except for the fact that in actual political life a capitalist society seems to guarantee religious freedom which cannot be offered by a marxist society, since marxist doctrine has itself grown into a political ideology of a religious nature. But I want to emphasize that the freedom of a capitalist society should never be identified with a true christian option.

Instead, I want to put forward that the christian conception of labour is not a vague moral sentiment but a clear reality, which reflects the biblical concepts of justice, harmony, and love. To the extent that socioeconomic organization is based on a marxist or a capitalist conflict model, alternatives must be pointed out. It cannot be denied that different socioeconomic

parties may have legitimate divergent interests, but it is
essential to attempt to place these interests *a priori* under the
unity of the law of God. The conflict between capital and labour
is a faulty structure that urgently needs to be changed. Both
employers and employees must begin to share the conviction
that labour, if seen in the light of the biblical concept of
responsible stewardship, is harmonious in nature. The
implications of this for socioeconomic institutional and labour
organizations at a microlevel will be dealt with later. First we
must take a look at current conflicting views with respect to the
place of labour in a technological society.

## Labour and technology

Does today's labour process not render a service to a materialist
expansion ideal? Does reflection on future problems not require
in the first place reflection on the place of labour? Does labour
only give support to the prevailing production system or does it
also contribute to human self-realization and spiritual
development? Does the power of current technocracy not lead to
the self-destruction of human labour? Is there any chance for a
human dimension in future labour conditions? Does the
economic expansion doctrine, fed by murderous competition,
not imply a barrier to labour satisfaction, to service toward
fellow human beings, and to fulfilment of one's total task in
God's kingdom?

These questions increasingly bother and puzzle us.
Socioeconomic and technological developments in the West
show a high degree of interwovenness and complexity. Instead
of simple handicraft and surveyable production, more and more
mechanization and automation take place. Consequently, man
is losing contact with the work of his hands or the work of his
head. He has become a small and neglected cog in an extensive,
dynamic social wheel. The results of his labour are hidden from
him and the societal meaning of labour disappears from his
range of vision. The ethics of labour is moving toward a crisis.

Increased productivity from mechanization and automation
to some extent also implies a threat to employment. It is Dennis
Gabor's opinion, for instance, that large-scale production,
combined with mechanization and automation, will produce a

society in which leisure time becomes a major problem. He has
even designed a blueprint for the future, when nuclear wars,
overpopulation, and labour problems will become central
issues.

Present high unemployment rates seem to support Dennis
Gabor's forecasts. In my opinion, however, it is hardly
convincing that postwar mechanization and automation are the
basic causes of the current employment situation. From the
time of the industrial revolution it has been realized that
industrialization and mass production satisfy a constantly
growing demand for commodities. Despite some recessions, the
overall pattern has been one of greater welfare and increased
employment.

Admittedly, in the administrative sector the computer has
taken over many mind-numbing activities, but at the moment
this is not the sector with the highest unemployment. As a
matter of fact, automation has had many positive effects on
employment opportunity in other sectors. What must be asked
is whether mind-numbing labour should be continued at the
expense of creative labour. It is clear that it is extremely difficult
to create simultaneously profitable and creative labour
conditions. Several social scientists consider modern
technological development a serious threat to man who becomes
a slave of the machine or computer. To counter this, increasing
emphasis is put on creative activities outside normal jobs. Even
a call for a theology of leisure time instead of a theology of labour
is made.

It is important to note that mechanization and automation
are not the only fundamental causes of structural
unemployment, unless economic growth stops. In a growing
economy, the demand for products will create new jobs; during
a recession, mechanization and automation will lead to
unemployment. This is precisely what we are now facing. For
that reason, the problem of economic growth, both nationally
and internationally, is of major significance. I will return to this
later.

Suffice it to say for the moment that labour, leisure time,
technology, and growth are concepts to be considered in close
relation to each other.

There is good reason why social ideologies like marxism and
neomarxism place so much emphasis on human labour and

freedom; for man should not become an extension piece of dead capital or lifeless machinery. According to Marx, alienation is the greatest evil in society, because it makes human labour meaningless and affects human dignity. He advocates a different view of labour, to create a new realm of freedom in which man may hunt and fish. Obviously, this utopia can only be attained by complete destruction of the capitalist order which oppresses man. After such a revolution, alienation in the sense of an artificial separation between human physical and spiritual resources will be overcome and the realm of freedom will set in.

The neomarxist Herbert Marcuse takes essentially the same standpoint, except that in his opinion, at present labourers are not at the lowest point of disaster; they are at the peak of well-being. Today, labourers have become slaves of their own welfare and a real liberation will be possible only when man is able to break away from the pinching strings of a consumer society. A utopian life of singing, playing, and dancing can be realized only once the dominance of our production technology is broken down. On the basis of today's welfare society, man should be able to attain a utopia in which he will be released from all coercive labour, and be "at play."

Another important neomarxist of the Frankfurt School, Jürgen Habermas, claims that technology, as long as it is geared to submission of and dominance over nature, by its very nature can hardly be changed via technical means. To abandon technology would also be impossible, since it is a result of human culture and creativity. Technology and science have become ideologies. In modern society, even the political process is unable to control technological forces, because democratic power is more oriented to solving *ad hoc* problems than to controlling science and technology. However, according to Habermas, technology is neither a given nor a fate, at least not as long as man strives toward a liberation process in which communication and social interaction take predominance over science and technology. This fuzzy utopia is to ignite a radical process of liberation today. It is Habermas's opinion that a change may take place so that *homo ludens* (man-at-play) may replace *homo faber*.

These marxist and neomarxist ideas illustrate once more that labour ethics, technology, and socioeconomic developments are

very closely linked together. Before developing concrete
christian guidelines it is necessary to see what the Bible says
about the place of labour in human life.

## *Labour and the Bible*

The biblical message is that man is not an autonomous being
but God's viceroy on earth. Man has the arduous and important
task to employ the treasures of creation in honour of the Lord
and for the salvation of his neighbour. To implement this task,
he has received many gifts or talents and, although these gifts
are affected by the fall into sin, basically the original task has not
changed since creation. Faithful labour definitely has a
profound meaning, even if much labour does not lead to direct,
observable results. The field of labour is not neutral. In this area
also man is a fully responsible being.

It should be noted that the task of man is not limited to paid
labour. Unpaid labour is not inferior to paid labour; faithful
labour is never inferior. Many activities outside the normal job
situation, such as church activities, social activities, domestic
work, and voluntary work, are equally important. From a
biblical point of view, the distinction between paid and unpaid
work is not relevant.

The Bible does not provide an extensive, all-embracing
doctrine of labour to be applied to every labour situation; it
provides the background and perspective for all faithful labour.
It may therefore be meaningful to formulate a set of criteria by
which the value and meaning of labour in concrete situations
can be judged.

1. Labour is a means for a meaningful development of the earth.
Man is a steward on earth with a great responsibility to the Lord,
his fellowmen, nature, and himself. Clearly, the fall into sin
exerted a destructive influence, but through Christ Jesus the
original human task has been restored, so that labour renders a
service to the coming kingdom of God. This implies that labour
may never be a vehicle for a materialistic expansion motive;
instead, it has to be a concrete signpost of a christian ethics
characterized by love of neighbour, truth, moderation, contact
with fellowmen, and justice.

2. The fall has left deep traces: work and sweat still go hand in hand despite optimism for a better future. The earth will never be a utopia. Work and labour are necessary to make a living. Work should provide man with a salary high enough to satisfactorily carry out his task in God's kingdom. The Bible does not supply us with an extensive distribution theory for income, but normally speaking everyone should have sufficient to live (a minimum threshold), while unlimited accumulation of income and wealth (a maximum threshold), should be discouraged. The difference between these two thresholds has to be distributed fairly and equitably, taking into account work conditions and responsibilities.

3. Much work has to be carried out to counteract the negative social consequences of the fall, for example, by the police, the army, social workers, and through medical services. Here also, moderation is more pertinent than utopian optimism. The battle against injustice, egoism, exploitation, and oppression can be considered an important motive for human labour in society.

4. Any expansionist optimism is contradictory to the biblical view of man as a pilgrim traveling toward a better homeland. During this pilgrimage, preaching the Gospel is a prerequisite. Man should not be dominated by restless work. God has proclaimed a rest for his children, under his vine and his figtree, as a reflection of the eternal rest awaiting the believer. Neglect of neighbour and dulled creativity may never be the ethical price for an overassessment of paid labour. Therefore, a production process should not render man a slave, but should stimulate responsibility, creativity, and social communication. Otherwise, we will ultimately arrive at the joyless economy recently described by T. Scitovsky.


## Labour in a christian view of society

What do the foregoing criteria for a biblical view of labour mean for a christian view of society? Much can be said about this. I will restrict myself to four themes, however.

1. *Labour and harmony-conflict models*

Everyone has a task in God's kingdom. God's law is valid for all human beings, though obviously the concrete application may vary, depending on the person, position, and talents. A main point in christian labour ethics is that labour is related to man's service to God and his neighbour. Therefore, to accept absolute opposition or conflict between employers and employees, between capital and labour, is a denial of the universal validity of this christian ethics. An institutionalized social structure based on the notion of a fundamental conflict between various groups and partners in society is itself in conflict with the unity of God's call for a harmonious social structure.

It is my deep conviction that such a conflict approach will lead to disastrous polarization. The universal biblical mandate implies a call for cooperation between employers, employees, government, and consumers whose various interests can be weighed against each other. To prevent a centrally controlled socioeconomic structure and a continuously conflicting social structure, I would like to make a plea for an institutionalized social structure which is based on sectoral cooperation and organization of all social partners. Such decentralized cooperation on a private basis at the sectoral level might lead to a socioeconomic structure which more adequately reflects harmony and responsibility.

This kind of organization would require a sectoral institution in which, not under compulsion but in freedom and cooperation, arrangements can be made with respect to future technology, new products, environmental policies, energy preservation, quality of work, and mutual competition. A curb on competition (for example, via some sort of indicative planning for goals at a decentralized level) would especially open many opportunities for socioeconomic development in which man is fully responsible and in which the value of labour really counts.

A model of cooperation does not solve all macro-problems of labour and technology, but I am convinced that such a structure is worth further consideration. There is no need to consider our present socioeconomic competitive structure with its many negative repercussions as irreversible. Earlier societies (like the medieval with its guilds) demonstrate that other meaningful structures are possible. In my opinion, organic socioeconomic institutional organization, based on normative cooperation between partners, is an authentic biblical alternative.

## 2. *Labour and micro-responsibility*

Today increasing interest in the quality of work and labour
conditions exists. A well-known example is provided by J.
Galtung's *On the Future of Human Society*. There are many
complaints about the quality of work: dehumanized conditions,
modern computer slavery, lack of social contact, and so forth.
These complaints must be taken seriously but, at the same time,
it should not be forgotten that labour conditions used to be
much worse, especially before and during the industrial
revolution. However, I am convinced that there is an urgent
need for work situations which are marked by creativity,
inventiveness, a sense of responsibility, and social contact.

Marxists and neomarxists frequently use the term *alienation*
to express that our privately based competitive economic
structure destroys favourable labour conditions. However,
despite the frequent use of this term, they display a striking lack
of insight into the real causes and the real existence of
alienation. This vaguely defined word is hardly subjectable to
empirical tests; it merely serves as an ideological attempt to
camouflage lack of empirical insight into actual labour
conditions. It would probably be better to forget the term and
speak of work "attractiveness" which might be operationalized
by means of the above-mentioned normative notions of degrees
of creativity, inventiveness, responsibility, and possibility for
social contact.

How can the quality of work be improved so that these
normative conditions are fullfilled? Conflict ideologists will
again answer that a class struggle or a dialectic emancipation
strategy combined with democracy at the microlevel are
essential ingredients for a new way of living and working.
However, these ideas do not take into account the biblical
notion of duties rather than rights, labour tasks rather than
labour rights.

I am convinced that broader participation by labourers at
various stages of the decision and production process would be
meaningful. A higher degree of participation might increase
labour satisfaction and stimulate the call for renovation and
development as it is incorporated in the christian concept of
labour. Instead of a liberal capitalist notion of labour as a
disutility, the high position of labour would thus be

emphasized. Instead of a socialist view of labour, in which central planning and democracy dominate individual initiatives, responsible stewardship should be stressed. It is my conviction that good labour conditions are based on participation and responsibility for all categories of people involved in the production process, given the normative structure of authority and management in an enterprise. I want to emphasize that this implies that a person should not necessarily identify himself with the objectives of an enterprise; a worker must carry out his God-given responsibility and does not necessarily equate this responsibility with that of the firm. An outgrowth would be properly functioning consultation between all partners, good information processing, stimulation of individual initiative, confirmation of self-respect and responsibility, joint reflection on new products, on new technologies, and on externalities, critical reflection on advertising, and attention to the social repercussions of private activities. This way, a flexible structure of participation may be more satisfactory than formal democracy at the enterprise level. The biblical call for responsible stewardship may thus find room to show to full advantage.

### 3. *Labour and unemployment*

Many industrialized countries are confronted with serious unemployment, from 6 to 10 percent. This situation may lead to a new depression. It should be remembered, however, that in the period before the industrial revolution an unemployment rate of 25 percent was no exception. This is not to deny that the present high rate is very unfavourable, because it prevents men from performing their tasks with regard to society and family.

Some social scientists have recently introduced the notion of the *right to work* for everybody. Such a right is a loose concept, because it presupposes an authority which provides a right to jobs. This would necessarily require a centrally controlled labour system, which has not yet been achieved even in communist countries. Further, such a right also presupposes the right to make use of it, so that the "right to work" would justify ethically unacceptable actions such as strikes and obstinate withdrawal from the labour force. What should be stressed instead is a call for faithful labour. This implies that society must try to create sufficient jobs for all its members. The creation of jobs is not only the responsibility of the government, but of entrepreneurs as well.

In addition to greater responsibility for creating jobs (by supplying job opportunities on the labour market), the responsibility for taking a job (by seeking jobs on the labour market) also has to be pointed out. The latter implies higher professional or even geographic mobility, stimulated by new educational programs. This also requires greater attractiveness in labour conditions as discussed above.

Earlier I pointed out that current unemployment is mainly a result of structural factors caused by international developments (such as the oil crisis and the energy situation). Further stimulation of economic growth might perhaps lead to a short-run solution to unemployment, but it would lead to a much more serious long-term ecological problem: the so-called "law of conservation of disaster." For that reason, some claim that economic growth should not be stimulated; that instead of creating new jobs, existing jobs have to be redistributed; and that there should be a guaranteed income for everyone.

However, redistribution of jobs does not lead to a solution to unemployment; it will generally stimulate further unemployment. The rise in labour costs as a result of partial jobs, and the maintenance of the *status quo* will hinder the dynamic development of an economy, so that in the long run the economic situation may even get worse. Moreover, it is not clear who should take responsibility for such redistribution, unless a centrally controlled economy would be accepted. I see no objection to public investments in order to create new jobs, but this should only take place when private enterprise itself does not succeed in creating them. A good starting point for a public policy for this purpose would be to accept that everything which can be done on a private basis should be done on a private basis. Sphere sovereignty is important to maintain a proper distinction between the private and the public sector.

The notion of a *guaranteed income* suffers from the same disadvantages. It is a hedonist idea, more in tune with a conception of man as being at play than being a steward who should also support himself. The artificial distinction implied here between creative leisure activity and tedious labour is not in harmony with the biblical norms for the quality of labour and human tasks. A guaranteed income also implies that a central authority (the government) is the distributor of both jobs and income. Such socioeconomic organization will stand in the way of a normative human performance of tasks.

To improve the present labour situation will require an interplay of two elements: first, it will have to be recognized that labour is not just a cost component, a disutility, but has a normative value going beyond production; that it is a fully cultural activity to honour the Lord and to serve fellowmen; and that in order to carry out this mandate, labourers should not lose their jobs too easily; second, it will have to be acknowledged that labour is by no means a tool for becoming as rich as possible, but provides a financial basis for all personal and family activities; and that a certain moderation in salary claims would be a good stimulus to break down the trend for more capital-intensive production processes.

### 4. *Labour and adjusted technology*

Unlimited stimulation of economic growth will bring about serious ecological problems. Apart from that, such stimulation would not testify to responsible stewardship. What to do in this situation?

Two possibilities are open to stimulate employment: first, increase production; and second, encourage labour-intensive production processes.

I would like to emphasize that a production increase is meaningful only if a set of complementary conditions is satisfied, such as constraint on the environment, energy, natural resources, the third world, and physical-spatial situations. When growth can be realized within these constraints, no objection to further production increase should exist. It is clear, however, that such increase should be allowed only in certain areas. Hence the term *selective growth*. Further, production increase should be such that labour-intensive processes are stimulated. Obviously, this requires an adjusted technology which no longer makes man a slave of the machine or the computer, but which allows him to be what he should be: a responsible steward. Barry Commoner put it this way: if we want to find the way to survival, then we have to find out how to manage technology according to the limits of nature and how to curb our economic wants within these limits.

I believe that a more holistic view of and approach to

economic, social, ecological, and technological problems is necessary if we are to control them. Efficiency criteria by themselves no longer hold; attention should also be paid to man-adjusted technology (frequently on a small scale), simple technology, flexible and labour-intensive technology, differentiated and creative technology, and so forth. I am convinced that a more holistic approach would be a tremendous challenge to christian science.

Let me try to illustrate this with some examples. Stimulation of environmental management by such means as environmental protection measures and recycling activities falls within the limits sketched here, especially because many of these activities are labour intensive, while not mind numbing. Urban renovation, residential rehabilitation, and landscape management in general are creative and labour intensive, requiring new small-scale technology to preserve historically and culturally valuable places and to satisfy ecological restraints.

Technocrats would probably say that many current problems are purely technical in nature and can be solved in the future. I don't share this opinion, at least not as long as technology itself is kept out of the discussion and is considered a foundation for the social sciences. In a holistic view of the world, technology also should be analyzed very critically, otherwise it might solve one problem while bringing about several others, as we have learned from bitter experience since the second world war.

A biblical view of human tasks and human responsibility with respect to social cooperation and participation is a prerequisite for a harmonious socioeconomic revival of a broken world.

# 4 *The Future of Labour**

*by Sander Griffioen*

## Introduction

This essay will not folllow the example of those which start with
long, space-consuming apologies for the fact that they do not
deal extensively with all the details of the subject matter.
Instead, my introduction will be limited to two remarks about
the title.

Firstly, in a paper of this length it is clear that the subject
cannot be given exhaustive treatment. Secondly, the term
*labour,* which refers mainly to the world of paid employment—
jobs—has been preferred to *work,* which in recent discussions
has tended to be given a broader meaning.

## Dialectics of labour

In western socioeconomic history there is a striking ambivalence
in the modern attitude toward labour. On the one hand, we love

---

* *Lecture presented at the Niagara summer conference sponsored by the Association for the Advancement of Christian Scholarship, August 1977.*

it and we praise it; on the other, we try to use as little of it as
possible. This constant oscillation has been an important feature
of western history since the Middle Ages.

I wonder if any other era has granted such a high status to
labour as ours. It may be equally difficult to find another culture
that has gone farther in downgrading it. At the end of this
section I shall try to prove that these two extreme attitudes are
connected; that the glorification and the depreciation, so to
speak, are facets of one and the same thing.

In a traditional world, man's place in society depends only to
a limited extent on what he does or does not do. Far more
important than personal achievements are the communities to
which one belongs for a lifetime: the family, clan, tribe, local
community, church. As we all know, these communities have
lost their central place in modern life. The clans and tribes have
disappeared; the family, though vitally important, is
endangered; while the churches no longer dominate either city
or village life.

The point is that, by and large, today labour has taken the
place of those communities just mentioned. This certainly did
not happen overnight; it was the result of a process lasting
centuries. Instead of being determined mainly by birth and
baptism, the individual's place within society became
determined first of all by his personal achievements. It is not by
what one is, but by what one does, that civil society measures
the value of its individual members.

This process should not be seen as entirely negative. It broke
the former power of the nobility by doing away with its most
important prerogatives and privileges and it freed economic
life, strangled as it was by a host of worn-out regulations. The
triumph of the labour principle surely had something of the
promise of the prophet: "They shall build houses and inhabit
them . . . they shall not build and another inhabit . . . my
chosen shall long enjoy the work of their hands." (Isaiah 65:2lf;
R.S.V.)

But the poison entered, as always, with the exaggeration.
The primacy of productive labour was not only directed against
the remnants of a feudal society; it also worked against those
who could not, for one reason or another, "achieve": the old, the
poor, and the unemployed.

Admittedly, much has changed since the nineteenth century,

when bourgeois society was at its height. Financially the old and the unemployed are better off than ever before. It would be ungrateful not to see a blessing in this. The problem, however, is that this blessing stays within the sphere of distribution, leaving the idol of production untouched.

This predicament comes out most sharply in its relation to the elderly. While in cultures such as Israel during biblical times wisdom and experience were held in high esteem and the old received a special, privileged status exactly because of their experience (which is still reflected in the word *elder*), in our world the aged feel left alone, excluded, superfluous. No longer "members" of the work force, they feel that they live at the expense of "society" and that their lives can only be justified in terms of the work they accomplished during their "productive" years.

The same holds for the unemployed. In ancient Greece, only those who did not have to work were considered true citizens. We should not defend that. The Bible never speaks in such terms. But in modern times we have come close to the other extreme. While in classical civilization those who worked for a living were rated as second-class citizens, today the opposite is frequently the case. Rosenstock-Huessy gives a telling definition of real citizenship, which he presented at a conference he attended in 1939: "A citizen is a man who is profitably employed."[1] The obvious implication is that all those who are not gainfully employed—the old, the homemakers, the unemployed—are not genuine citizens! In this decade we don't encounter similar statements as easily as in the 1930s.[2] But that should not lead anyone to underrate the burden that is upon the shoulders of those excluded from productive work. Investigations show that losing self-respect is the greatest single problem facing them.

For those who are "gainfully employed," on the other hand, the job has become central to their daily lives, while family life, community life, church work, etc., increasingly are relegated to a secondary place, that is, to their free time "after work," when there is competition from leisure activities such as watching TV or engaging in sports and recreation.

If productive labour is really so precious to our civilization, why is it so ill-treated?

With regard to the negative side, for the moment it will

suffice to look at the conveyor belt and at what it has done to the workers. Its inhuman effects are immortalized in Charlie Chaplin's film, *Modern Times*. This film was made in the thirties. Much later, Chaplin recounted what led him to make it. He got the idea from a bright young reporter at the *New York World:*

> Hearing that I was visiting Detroit, he told me of the factory-belt system there—a harrowing story of big industry luring healthy young men off the farms, who, after four or five years of the system, became nervous wrecks. It was this conversation which gave me the idea for *Modern Times*.[3]

The father of the conveyor-belt system was Frederick Taylor, the American engineer who did his most important investigations during the early years of this century. He initiated the time studies of all the different bodily movements that make up a task. His aim was to enhance efficiency by reducing the work of the labourers to a well-defined set of recurrent movements, an ideal partly realized with the introduction of conveyor belts and assembly lines.

Taylor is often depicted as the enemy of the working class, a man whose goal it was to squeeze as much as possible out of the workingman. This was not the image he had of himself. It was his honest intention to help overcome the adversary relationship between labour and management. It was his conviction that the interests of management and labour could and should be harmonized.[4] The way to harmony was seen to be through the promotion of the productivity of labour. In his main work, *Principles of Scientific Management,* time and again a secularized puritan work ethic comes to the surface. Taylor wanted to honour labour by streamlining its performance and excluding idleness and irresponsibility. However, this way of honouring labour is self-contradictory. Streamlining of work done by the worker leads to the point where eventually a machine can take over. A steelworker, whose story is the opening one in Studs Terkel's famous book *Working,* remarks:

> You're doing this manual labor and you know that technology can do it. (Laughs.) Let's face it, a machine can do the work of a man; otherwise they wouldn't have space probes. Why can we send a rocket ship that's unmanned and yet send a man in a steel mill to do a mule's work?[5]

The example of Taylor's scientific management suggests that the two sides, the idolization and the depreciation of human labour, belong together. His conviction, that since labour is so precious it ought to be managed with the greatest possible care, has placed the worker in a position of competition with lifeless machinery!

Philosophers have a term for this kind of inherent contradiction. They call it a *dialectical relation*. One might suspect this to be another philosopher's trick, to make people believe that a mystery is explained by simply giving it a name. In this case, however, philosophy is of great help, for it shows that the glorification of productive work and its factual mistreatment are not two unrelated factors but, in fact, stem from one common root.

Insight into the dialectic of labour may lead to other discoveries as well. It helps to detect similar tensions within other cultures—cultures which, for all their distinctiveness, in important respects live out of the same roots as the western world. Soviet Russia is a case in point. On the one hand, one is struck in soviet communism by an exuberant glorification of labour, that nowhere finds a clearer expression than in those well-known paintings and posters showing members of the working class, standing in the light of the morning sun to greet the new day in which, once again, labour will be all in all.[6] This ethos, on the other hand, did not prevent Lenin, shortly after the revolution, from defending and introducing some of Frederick Taylor's ideas on efficiency.[7] It is interesting to note that Chaplin's *Modern Times,* thought by many Americans to be only an indictment of the American way of life, greatly confused its Russian audiences. As recorded in a study on Chaplin:

> Most significant, perhaps, was the Russian reaction. At its Moscow showing, according to an article in the *New York Times,* the film was not considered much of an aid to the cause of the revolution. The Moscow public greeted the conveyor-belt scene in stony silence (perhaps because of the turn to conveyor-belt production in soviet industry and the new speed-up order.)[8]

The American steelworker whom I quoted earlier has rightly seen that this type of communism offers no alternative to American capitalism:

Why is it that the communists always say they're for the workingman, and as soon as they set up a country, you got guys singing to
tractors? They're singing about how they love the factory. That's
where I couldn't buy communism. It's the intellectuals' utopia, not
mine. I cannot picture myself singing to a tractor, I just can't.
(Laughs.) Or singing to steel.[9]

## A glance into the future

It goes without saying that the replacement of workmen by
machines may well lead to unemployment. Nevertheless, in the
thinking of (mainstream) economists and politicians this so-
called "technological unemployment" has never had a large
place. Quite often they argue that, although technology may
replace a certain group of workers, it will also provide new jobs,
given the simple fact that the new machinery itself has to be
produced. This, of course, is true. But there is no inherent
reason why the two should balance. There is no guarantee that
the new technology will create as much employment as it
replaces. In fact, when we look back at what has happened
during the last twenty years, we see that in none of the western
countries employment in the industrial sector has grown
impressively. (Actually, in quite a few branches of industry,
employment has fallen.) There has been, instead, a gradual shift
from the industrial sector to the sector of services. It's there that
the bulk of new jobs has been created.

Examples of services are the police force, the army, health
services, research, education, but also the world of trade and
finance. In most of the western economies, it is here, far away
from the conveyor belt, that more than 50 percent of the labour
force is employed. Industry no longer is typical of the modern
economy. "Industrial workers now constitute only about 25
percent of the workers and their number is shrinking fast."[10]
With a view to this state of affairs new concepts have been
introduced, notably "service economy" and "postindustrial
society," the last word owing its specific colour to the
futurologists of the Hudson Institute in New York: Herman
Kahn, Daniel Bell, and others.

In one of the recent publications of the Hudson Institute,
Daniel Bell (who is said to have invented the phrase "post-

industrial society") predicts that the service sector's share in total employment will rise from its present just under 60 percent to almost 70 percent in the 1980s.[11] Small wonder that this type of publication does not dwell long on the threat of growing technological unemployment: there is too much confidence that any decline in industrial employment will be offset by enough new jobs in the services to satisfy those who are flexible and creative enough to adapt to new circumstances.[12]

I do not share the optimism of the Hudson Institute. It might well be that the growth in the service sector already is approaching its limits and it may even become increasingly difficult to maintain the level of services we have attained.

In the first place, it is only too likely that in the years ahead enormous sums of money will be needed to pay for energy projects: in Canada, hydro projects, tar sands projects, pipelines, and so on. It is probable that this will leave less money available for services. Some years ago Donald McDonald, then Canadian federal minister of energy, predicted that in the next ten years the proportion of the gross national product going toward energy development would nearly double compared to the 1960s. And he added, "In human terms, that would mean less capital proportionally to build new housing, new schools, and other needed social developments."

The Committee for Justice and Liberty before the National Energy Board of Canada rightly drew attention to this statement.[13] It is true that we are facing decisions here that are likely to have a significant effect on the employment situation. In his open letter to the Canadian Minister of Indian Affairs and Northern Development, justice Thomas Berger pointed out that once a pipeline like the proposed Mackenzie Valley pipeline is built, not more than about 250 people would be needed to operate it.[14] Here one sees that a shift away from the labour-intensive services sector can very well lead to a net loss of employment opportunities.

For yet another reason one should be skeptical about the prediction of a steadily developing postindustrial society offering ever more employment in its services sector. In a time of persistent cost inflation it is important to note that the possibility of cutting costs through increased mechanization is the most limited precisely in this sector. In order to survive, there often seems to be just one way left—the one the Canadian hotel industry has taken. A recent survey reported:

> Canada's hotels have tried to counteract rapidly rising costs by
> cutting down on services, a four-year study . . . suggests. And
> reducing services in the industry usually means employing fewer
> people. . . . repair and maintenance expenses in 1975 and 1976
> decreased by 7 per cent while other costs were rising.[15]

Schools, universities, public health services, etc., are in a
better position insofar as they can shift the burden of the rising
outlays to the government's budget, but increasingly here too
the crunch is felt. One only has to take a glance at the
phenomenal cost of the payroll of a modern university to realize
that the period of rapid expansion belongs to the past.

By way of a conclusion, we may say that without considerable
efforts unemployment is likely to rise. According to Arthur M.
Okun, in the USA it takes about 4 percent real growth in the
gross national product to keep unemployment from rising.[16] In
1977, the Organisation for Economic Co-operation and
Development (OECD) calculated that a growth rate above 5
percent is needed to stop the rise in Canada's unemployment,
while it expected the actual growth rate not to exceed 4 percent
in the years to come.[17] This drives home one point in particular.
The prospect of a society growing ever more distinctively
postindustrial in character, with a service sector ready to offer
stable employment to all who wish, is not more than a pipe
dream of certain futurologists, based upon expectations raised
in the sixties when almost everything seemed possible. On one
occasion, in 1968, the Council of Economic Advisors to the
president of the USA triumphantly declared:

> No longer do we view our economic life as a relentless tide of ups
> and downs. No longer do we fear that automation and technical
> progress will rob workers of jobs rather than help us to achieve
> greater abundance. No longer do we consider poverty and
> unemployment permanent landmarks on our economic scene.[18]

## Magic solutions

If the employment prospects really are so bleak, what can be
done? Should we sit back and say that we must learn to see our
present-day unemployment as being "normal"? That we
mustn't panic? After all, these unemployed are financially much

better off than their predecessors of the thirties. Or should we passionately refuse to see the new predicament as being close to normality?

In this section, I'll limit myself to examining two challenging answers to these questions. Both say that we cannot afford anything less than radical solutions. The solutions they propose are certainly radical: "magic" one could call them; and, moreover, they are conflicting!

The people adhering to the first view argue as follows. While we are so keen about natural energy nowadays, we have never learned to fully tap the "most important of all resources: the initiative, imagination and brain power of man himself."[19] Is it not a shame, in fact a cultural sin of the first order, to pay millions of people to stay out of work, many of them creative, young people? "Some 7m of the rich world's young people cannot find jobs," read the first sentence of a survey that appeared not long ago.[20] According to John Eleen, director of research for the Ontario Federation of Labour, a society that tolerates an 8 percent unemployment rate is a sick society, and "those who brought about such a state of affairs are guilty of irresponsibility bordering on criminal negligence."[21]

But there is more involved than the awful waste of human capabilities. Unemployment is also a major source of alienation. Being on the dole means losing one's self-respect and not being able to contribute to the common good and to feel needed and wanted in return.

It's felt that the prevailing government's policies to boost employment are far too lax. All adults have a basic right to a job and the government must go as far as possible in guaranteeing it, if necessary by creating jobs within its own domain.

Historically, the position here depicted is connected with certain types of socialism. You all know those pamphlets and posters advocating jobs for all! Socialists like to speak of the "dignity of work" and every adult's "right to work." The prime failure of individualistic capitalism is seen to lie in the fact that it is not able to ensure lasting full employment. Only by turning away from individualism can this be assured. One of the fathers of christian socialism expressed himself in 1912 in this way: if no other employment is available, the worker should be able to "fall back on the community itself for employment!"[22] Nowadays, instead of the phrase "to fall back on the community for employment," quite often the expression is used, "the government as the employer in last resort."

Before commenting, let us first hear the other view. In this view the right to a job is given much less emphasis. Instead, the right to food and to the other basic necessities of life is given priority. In fact, its adherents argue that labour and income ought to be disjoined. Instead of attempting to act as the employer in last resort, the government would do well to guarantee to all its subjects a decent income, irrespective of the question whether they work or not.[23] Or, to put it in plain language, what is proposed is nothing less than severing the tie between income and labour.

The deeper objective is to make work a goal in itself, simply by taking away the necessity to work. This will help, it is hoped, to eradicate those remnants of the so-called protestant work ethic that are engrained in all of us. It is the overwhelming sense of duty that makes us all prone to guilt feelings when we do not produce sufficiently. This passion to be productive is the counterpart of the growing inability to be silent, to listen, to enjoy oneself. It must be crucified because it fuels the economic rat race and deforms the human personality.

A Dutch newspaper accused one of the champions of this viewpoint of not understanding even the ABC of economics.[24] That, perhaps, is exactly what you already suspected. However, in this circle we do find some fairly well elaborated ideas concerning the economic implications and consequences.

A distinction is made between one sector of the economy which will remain market and profit oriented, and another which will be dominated by nonprofit-making cooperatives. Those people who are not satisfied with their guaranteed income can seek employment in the market sector. In the cooperatives no wages are paid.

Who will be prepared to work if it does not add anything to his income? That truly is a valid question. We should note, however, that to this utopia belongs the expectation that through education people will learn to choose self-fulfilling work.

Nobody will deny that the proposal under discussion is radical. It offers a twofold solution to the unemployment problem. In the first place, it would take away from the unemployed the burden of feeling unproductive, because under the new conditions productive work in the traditional meaning of the word would become the exception rather than the norm. In the second place, a redistribution of existing work is envisaged, because not many people would put so much time into their work as presently is required for a full-time job.

I'm convinced that both proposals discussed here only offer would-be, magic solutions.[25] Their character is essentially a-historical; they do not build upon real possibilities present within the given constellation. By the same token, both views tend to underrate the efforts needed for breaking away from trends that have shaped so much of our western history. To take the first example, making the government into the employer in last resort as such does not guarantee a genuine liberation of work from the dialectic of labour mentioned earlier. The same holds true of the second proposal. (Ironically enough, it might be necessary under the "new" conditions to assign tasks, simply to get the necessary work done.) Setting up production cooperatives might be an important step in improving employment policies, especially among the urban poor. Nowhere is the failure of traditional employment policies becoming so clear as in the urban jungles. In a city like Chicago, to mention only one example, nearly half the black and Hispanic youth is out of work, while another large percentage holds only poorly paid jobs. In such a situation, setting up small-size production cooperatives looks more promising than making extra investments in large-scale plants of standardized products. One reason is that the cooperatives are more likely to foster a sense of belonging and thus to solicit responsibility and initiative on the part of the workers.

Such an approach, however, has a chance of success only if it is geared to what is already alive or could be revitalized in existing institutions and structures such as the family, neighbourhood, church organizations, voluntary organizations, and ethnic groups. I want to stress that counteracting the dismal trends in large urban centres demands more than such magic solutions as a dissociation of work and income. It requires painstaking, patient work. It requires an attitude, entirely different from the impatience of the revolutionary, of respect for what is alive within the existing structures. Here, I think, the words of Groen van Prinsterer hold true, that every genuine reform presupposes respect for the existing historical givens.[26]

## Called to serve

Once more we will return to the two magic solutions, but now with an eye to the dialectic introduced at the beginning of this essay.

First the full-employment champions. One of them described the promised land of full employment as a "humanistic capitalism" under which "there is full opportunity for every member (of society) to contribute to the society and to feel wanted and needed in return."[27] Beautiful words! Who does not know the desire to contribute to something greater than himself and to feel wanted and needed in return? In August 1977, a banner-wide headline in the *Toronto Star* read, "The hidden agony of Toronto's unemployed." It's not first of all their financial plight that distresses those who are jobless against their will, it was argued there. Rather, it is the feeling of being cut off from the possibility of contributing to "society"; it's the feeling of not being needed and wanted.

However, disregarding the deeper problems involved would be just as bad as ignoring the agony of the unemployed. It does not make sense to create jobs just for the sake of employment. It is madness to build houses, roads, expressways, you name it, primarily to satisfy people's need to feel wanted and needed. This is no less bizarre than defending Japanese whaling or the seal hunt in Newfoundland simply because of the employment involved in these projects.

Is not the deeper cause of the agony of the unemployed the premium placed nowadays on employment? Today only employment, productive labour, seems to be able to secure us a place within society, to make us into useful, respected citizens. Why do we despair when losing our job? Is it not because we are cut off from the future we had wanted to build with our own hands?

It's here that the dialectical counterpart enters into the picture. There is no doubt that those who stress so strongly the importance of labour quite often are almost indifferent to its content, quality, and direction. This became overwhelmingly clear to me while attending a "jobs-for-all" rally of the Communist Party of Canada. Everything that was being said that evening amounted to one fierce outcry against the economic system for not providing enough jobs. However, none of those present (and their number was not all that great because of a hockey game held the same evening) cared to ask, "What kind of work? What are meaningful employment opportunities? Which needs must be fulfilled? How do we tackle technological unemployment?"

Are Christians so much different from communists on this score?

Luther and Calvin stressed with strong conviction the principial equality of all sorts of labour before God's face. Remember Calvin's splendid words:

> Hence also will arise peculiar consolation, since there will be no employment so mean and sordid (provided we follow our vocation) as not to appear truly respectable, and be deemed highly important in the sight of god.[28]

These words surely have lost none of their value. They are open, however, to one peculiar misunderstanding, in that they might be taken to mean that it is not really important what occupation we choose, all types of work being equally suitable in working out one's calling. We might be led to think that it does not make much difference whether, for example, we engage in working with retarded children or in producing deodorants, as long as the work is done with the self-discipline and frugal self-effacement that have been ridiculed as the protestant or puritan work ethic.

Recently a Reformed theologian rightly spoke up against such a diluted understanding of the "divine calling." He warned that many of our present-day occupations do not really deserve the word *divine*. Referring to the "cultural mandate" to subdue and develop the earth, he argued that much economic activity is of such a nature that it simply cannot be seen as an obedient response to the mandate to develop creation.[29] We have as much reason to be wary of the so-called protestant work ethic as of the communist, socialist or liberal work ethic.[30]

This seems to leave only one alternative open: to take sides with those who want to free labour from its constraints, to transform it into an activity that is fully gratifying. But does not the meaning of labour become just as much distorted as in the case where the subjective desire to feel wanted and needed prevails? There certainly exists here a concern for the content of work, but in a peculiar way, aimed at the value it has in terms of the individual's self-development. It is my contention that service, not self-realization, is the inner destination of human labour.[31] Self-realization is, so to speak, a concomitant, or rather, a gift.[32] Where the gift is made into the sole meaning and end, labour turns into a self-centred activity, closed off against what Calvin Seerveld has graphically called "the reality of the rainbow" under which the Lord has placed the work of our hands, a reality that makes labour open up toward "praising-serving stewardship . . . touched by the certainty of the Final Jubilee."[33]

## The liberation of labour

Seeing the calling of labour should lead to a discerning of creational needs. H. van Riessen used to say that there will always be enough work left to be done in the world. Indeed, a shortage of job opportunities by no means implies that the task to develop creation is coming close to completion! Look, for instance, at modern farm life, where the promotion of efficiency has gone on at the expense of proper care for the soil, fruits, trees, and livestock. How much more time could be put in than actually is spent there! The same holds true for our villages and cities. Parts of them may have to be torn down and rebuilt in the future. Some time ago *The Economist* stated quite bluntly: "The number of modern buildings in London, for instance, that are distinguished for anything other than ugliness is trivial." Additional examples abound. One only has to look at the junk that leaves the factory gates, at the built-in obsolescence of products that are essential, at the poor quality of services, as well as at work conditions and at labour relations. How little of all this expresses unambiguously a divine calling!

Let us not forget that in a certain sense the odds are against anyone who takes his calling seriously. It has happened more than once that, after having introduced a christian approach to economic life, people tell me: "I have tried for a long time to arrange my business in accordance with christian principles, I have tried to be a steward as well as I could, but the economy does not seem to leave you the time and the space needed to work responsibly. Given the pressure of competition and the squeeze of inflation, the only way to survive seems to be to play it safe by complying with prevailing standards and customs."

Let me rephrase this complaint in my own words. The combined pressure of inflation and competition is such that it narrows down the fulness of economic life to one thing: economize or perish! The imperative under which we work, especially those employed in the industrial sector, is to cut down on costs as much as possible and to avoid everything that is not strictly necessary. Structural change must be legitimized by the productivity gains it brings about.

This constant pressure robs notions like "shalom for economic life," "harvest," and "jubilee" of their reality, or gives them the appearance of having no reality outside the private utopia of christian intellectuals.

The pressures on economic life certainly are not generated only by competition and inflation. There is a deeper restlessness engrained in our civilization. I'll try to elucidate this from one particular angle: our experience of time.

Somewhere in *Gulliver's Travels,* Gulliver is asked by the Lilliputians as to the function and importance of his watch.[34] On hearing Gulliver explain how much this watch means to him, they think it to be his personal god. Is not this the god of much of modern economic life? Does it not seem as though Benjamin Franklin's slogan, "Time is money," is inscribed above every factory gate? Inside the factory the prevailing time mode is abstract mechanical time, symbolized by the time clock and the stopwatch, made famous by Frederick Taylor's "scientific" management.

To put it more generally: nothing is given time to mature. In economic life the time horizon is so limited that a ten-year moratorium, as proposed in the case of the northern pipeline, is almost inconceivable.

Within this time horizon, labour does not have a real future, which can be seen very clearly in the way concepts like *efficiency* and *productivity* are geared to labour "saving." Enhancing the productivity of labour means using less labour time per product (a reduction of the time one worker spends on one product or on rendering one particular service). The time saved is relocated as leisure time, in an area entirely separated from the world of labour.

No societal group can be blamed exclusively for the malaise of economic life. Labour's preoccupation with more pay, shorter workweeks, and longer vacations is itself a reflex of the tyranny of mechanical time. Where the time clock and the rhythm of machines hold sway, the "liberation" of labour is narrowed down quite naturally to higher wages and more leisure time. Nor can the blame be placed exclusively on the managers, because they act under just as much pressure. Besides, the principles of their management stem from a spiritual tradition that since the Renaissance has dominated major parts of our culture.

To fight this giant, simple recipes and quick solutions will not do any good. It is the spirit of the times that has to be conquered. This can only be done by surrendering to Him who says: "I have overcome the world." (John 16:33) In a way, that is exactly what the Christian does every day. We have to acknowledge, however, that socioeconomic life is part of the battleground. Therefore, the freedom the Christian has gained in Christ should in a specific way become manifest in his labour.

Here the phrase "liberation of labour" is appropriate. These words have a modern ring, but they are at the same time firmly rooted in the Reformed tradition: as far back as 1903 J.C. Sikkel chose them as the title for what was to become his most important publication.[35]

The liberation meant here is a liberation from the pressures that hamper labour, that keep it from living up to its calling. But liberation for what? For becoming a self-centred, autonomous activity of the well-rounded individual? For becoming an instrument for bringing shalom to the world? No, it means liberation to serve! This liberation take place "under the cross." The false pretences so deeply engrained in "labour" and "work" must be crucified first. Only through this painful operation can labour be freed, freed to serve.[36] To depict the liberation of labour, Bob Goudzwaard has used the image of the sequence of Sunday followed by the workweek. In the secular conception of work, this order is reversed. The work of our hands and of our head is seen as the liberating, shalom-bringing force. So it is in the communist and socialist work ethic, no less than in the liberal-conservative work ethic with its myth of productive labour.

The Torah first says, "Remember the Sabbath day to keep it holy," and then adds, "Six days you shall labour and do all your work." Shalom thus precedes work and gives it its framework. In our society, however, everything is first of all concentrated on our restless pursuit of what we can produce through our own efforts![37]

And, in another place:

> Nevertheless, shalom is never attained in this way, for shalom is not the result of our work and our activities. Acceptance with God is the basis for our life and work![38]

What does this liberation mean concretely in the shop? Let me mention a few things. It means *time* in which the workers can take real responsibility; time for changing the rhythm of the machines, for adapting them to a human rhythm, instead of the other way around; time for making decisions about the nature and quality of the products; time also for making more use of the experience of older employees (rather than resorting to retirement schemes which sometimes specify that those who retire may not take up paid employment within five or ten years).

One way to approach these things is the way the Christian Labour Association of Canada has chosen. Listen to Calvin Seerveld's words:

> It is the promise of the CLAC not to be conservatistically opportunist in getting fringe benefits to compensate for drudgery, but to pledge to workmen and women to help change the labouring situation itself so that there can be a leisurable moment within the very task and so that "weekends" and vacations can become festive culminations of joy, like harvest upon one's labours.[39]

Is this so different from what certain secular movements propose, one might ask? No . . . and yes! In particular there are similarities with proposals of movements to improve quality of work life and to promote the humanization of work. This is fortunate enough! We have reason to be thankful that these movements are gaining so much ground nowadays. But there is also another side to it. The humanization of work is constantly in danger of becoming a human*ism* of work. It's easily confused with the attempt to make work a self-centred, autonomous activity, without worrying much about the inflationary effects of high standards of living, nor about the unemployed outside the factory gates.

It is, therefore, all-important to keep stressing the liberation *to serve.* Only then are we able to discern the rainbow of God's covenant stretched out over the work of our hands.

## Notes

1. Eugen Rosenstock-Huessy, *Der unbezahlbare Mensch* (Berlin: Vogt, 1955), last chapter.

2. The conference mentioned above took place in the USA. In some other countries, notably Germany and the USSR, the cult of labour was even stronger. One of the slogans of the national socialists was "Jeder echte Deutscher ist Arbeiter" [Every real German is a worker]. Below I make a few comments about Russia.

3. Charlie Chaplin, *My Life in Pictures* (London, Sydney, Toronto: Bodley Head, 1974), p. 257.

4. See, for instance, p. 23 of Frederick Taylor, *Principles of Scientific Management* (New York: Norton, 1967), written in 1911, where the fact is deplored that so many employers look upon the employees as antagonists, if not enemies, and where a plea is made for a "mutual confidence which should exist between a leader and his men, the enthusiasm, the feeling that they are all working for the same end and will share in the results."

5. Studs Terkel, *Working* (New York: Pantheon, 1974), p. xxxiii.

6. Marx himself inherited the bourgeois absolutization of productive labour. In the *German Ideology* (1846; Moscow: Progress, 1976), to give one example, he makes a distinction between individuals as they may appear in their own and other people's imagination and *as they really are,* i.e., as they operate, produce materially ["wie sie wirklich sind, d.h. wie sie wirken," *Karl Marx Frühe Schriften,* vol. 2 (Darmstadt: Cotta, 1971), p. 22]. In this matter, there exists one important difference, though, between Marx and soviet marxism. For Marx, under socialism labour would become a means rather than an end in itself. The end of Marx's socialism is the full, all-sided development of the social individual and the ultimate gate leading to it is . . . the shortening of the workday! [See especially the *Grundrisse* (1857-1859; New York: Vintage, 1974); see also Ed Vanderkloet's essay, "Why Work Anyway," elsewhere in this collection].

7. Cf. Daniel Bell, *Work and its Discontents: the Cult of Efficiency in America* (New York: League for Industrial Democracy, 1970), p. 41. Bell refers to

Lenin's speech on "Scientific Management and the Dictatorship of the Proletariat" (June 1919). It is well known that present-day Russian industry is in fact split up in two sectors, the one modern and efficient (armaments and other strategic industries), the other consisting of production units considerably more traditional and labour-intensive than their American counterparts. See, for instance, Hedrick Smith, *The Russians* (New York: Ballantine Books, 1976), pp. 285-319.

8. Theodore Huff, *Charlie Chaplin* (New York: Arno Press & New York Times, 1972), p. 256.

9. Terkel, *Working,* pp. xxxiv-v.

10. *The Economist,* 25 December 1976, p. 57.

11. "The Post-Industrial Society: Expectations for the 1970s and 1980s" in Herman Kahn, ed., *The Future of the Corporation* (New York: Mason & Lipscomb, 1974), p. 20.

12. Kahn foresees that in the longer run the computer revolution will bring about "enormous savings of labor," also in the services sector. To him, not unemployment, but rather the much shorter workweek presents the main challenge. What will man do with his free time? "Will he seek even more to test himself in the combat of sport, the risk of adventure or the challenge of exploration? Or will he be able and prefer to experience all of this—and more—through artificial stimulation?" Herman Kahn *et al., The Next Two Hundred Years: A Scenario for America and the World* (New York: Morrow, 1976), pp. 225-26.

13. *Final Argument,* submitted for the Committee for Justice and Liberty by John A. Olthuis before the National Energy Board in the Matter of the Mackenzie Valley Pipeline Hearings, Ottawa, 3 June 1977, p. 78. Available from CJL, 229 College Street, Toronto, Ontario, Canada M5T 1R4.

14. Published in Mr. Justice Thomas R. Berger, *Northern Frontier, Northern Homeland; The Report of the Mackenzie Valley Pipeline Inquiry,* vol. 1 (Ottawa: Printing and Publishing Supply and Services Canada, c. 1977.), p. xx.

15. *The Globe and Mail,* Toronto, 29 December 1977, p. B1.

16. Cf. Barry Commoner, *The Poverty of Power: Energy and the Economic Crisis* (New York: Alfred A. Knopf, 1976), p. 239.

17. *The Globe and Mail,* Toronto, 29 December 1977, p. 6.

18. Quoted by J. K. Galbraith, "The Trouble with Economists," *The New Republic,* 14 January 1978, p. 17.

19. E. F. Schumacher, "Philosophy of Work," *The Guide,* August-September 1977, p. 11. Quoting Schumacher here does not *per se* imply that his views are seen to fall under the category of magic solutions.

20. *The Economist,* 11 June 1977, p. 87.

21. Quoted by Ronald Anderson in his column in *The Globe and Mail,* Toronto, 3 August 1977, p. B2, entitled "A sick society."

22. Walter Rauschenbusch in *Christianizing the Social Order* (New York: Macmillan 1912); quoted in Lowell A. Hagan, "The Christian Socialism of Walter Rauschenbusch," (Toronto: Institute for Christian Studies, 1977), p. 53. (Mimeographed.)

23. Robert Theobald, one of the foremost proponents of this view, has proposed that the Employment Act of 1946 (USA) be amended into a "Right to Income Act" (cf. G.J. Leibrandt, *Automatisering en werkgelegenheid* [Automation and employment opportunity], inaugural address at the Free University of Amsterdam, 1965, p. 13).

24. *De Telegraaf,* 8 February 1975; written in reply to professor J. Kuiper of the Free University, who in a public speech had made a plea for a guaranteed income, basing himself primarily on Theobald's *Free Men and Free Markets* (New York: Anchor, 1965) Cf. *VU-Magazine,* March 1975, pp. 29-39.

25. I have left out of consideration those proposals for a guaranteed income that are not primarily concerned with employment and unemployment, but rather with eliminating red tape in the administration of existing social-welfare programs.

26. These lines are partly inspired by what I have read and heard about the work of the Voice of Calvary mission in poverty-stricken areas of Jackson, Mississippi. This work, led by John Perkins, entails the setting up of cooperatives, of model farms and of much more, all this being done with great concern for the spiritual redirection of the lives of those involved.

27. See John D. Rockefeller, III, *The Second American Revolution: Some Personal Observations* (New York: Harper and Row, 1973), chapter 10.

28. These are the last lines of book 3, chapter 10, of Calvin's *Institutes of the Christian Religion,* as translated by John Allen (Philadelphia: Presbyterian Board of Christian Education, 1936), vol. I, p. 791.

29. Cf. J. Douma, "De ethiek van de arbeid" [The ethics of labour], *Ambt en plicht* 24 (April 1977), pp. 97-99, and 24 (May 1977), pp. 110-112. These two articles are as rich as they are concise. See also note 36.

30. We owe to Richard Nixon a fine general formulation of the work ethic: "The 'work ethic' holds that labor is good in itself; that a man or a woman becomes a better person by virtue of the act of working. America's competitive spirit, the 'work ethic' of this people, is alive and well on Labor Day, 1971." (One of the mottoes to Terkel, *Working,* p. ix.)

31. I do not mean to say that with "service" the meaning of labour is exhausted. H. Evan Runner, in defining "office," mentioned "service" and "administration": "Office is not merely service (dienen); it is also administration" (bedienen); it is service of God and an administering of God's love and solicitude to the creature at the same time." In the next sentence "administration" is further clarified with the words "preserving and orderly form-giving." *The Relation of the Bible to Learning* (Toronto: Wedge, 1974), p. 147. It should be kept in mind that *calling* is a broader concept than *labour.*

32. Here H. van Riessen's remarks on the difference between an orientation in terms of "needs" and one in terms of "vocation" are pertinent: "in the former man chooses himself as the final goal of life; in the latter man renounces his own person in everything and is aware of the relation of responsibility towards God. This second viewpoint, however, does not imply that man has no needs. But they are of secondary importance, a concomitant, such as, e.g. self-realization, which is a concomitant phenomenon of the performance of the cultural task." *The Society of the Future* (Philadelphia: Presbyterian & Reformed, 1952), p. 255.

33. Calvin Seerveld, "The Unfulfilled Promise of the CLAC, in Edward Vanderkloet, ed., *A Christian Union in Labour's Wasteland* (Toronto: Wedge, 1978), p. 129.

34. Bell, *Work and its Discontents*, p. 5.

35. J.C. Sikkel, *Vrijmaking van den arbeid* [Liberation of labour] (Amsterdam, Pretoria: Höveker & Wormser, 1903).

36. One of the best essays on the biblical view of labour I know of is "De ethiek van de arbeid" [The ethics of labour], by professor Jochem Douma of Kampen (*Ambt en plicht*, April 1977 and May 1977). Cf. note 29. It stresses one important element that could not be taken into account in the present essay; namely, that the liberation of labour in Christ does not necessarily mean that the curse about which one reads in Genesis 3 will be entirely dissipated.

> Since through the cross Christ took all sin upon Himself, He also rescued all believers from the curse of labour of Genesis 3:17-19; for it no longer merely leads to sorrow, pain and fruitlessness; in following Christ we also experience its fruits: as servants of Christ we are able to come to terms with suffering. (*Ambt en plicht*, April 1977, p. 98.)

37. Bob Goudzwaard, *Aid for the Overdeveloped West* (Toronto: Wedge, 1975), p. 28.

38. *Ibid.*, p. 30.

39. Seerveld, "The Unfulfilled Promise of the CLAC," in Vanderkloet, ed., *A Christian Union in Labour's Wasteland*, p. 129.

# 5
# Toward a Society without a Perspective?*

*by Peter Nijkamp*

## Introduction

The period since the second world war is increasingly characterized by sharp contrasts. Never in the history of man has there been such impressive economic and technological progress nor, simultaneously, such a wide gap between rich and poor. With our present technological knowledge we are able to nourish astronauts in outer space under terrible conditions; meanwhile, however, in cities like Calcutta, thousands of people die from malnutrition. We are in search of living beings on other planets like Mars; yet we are barely interested in our own surroundings. We stimulate technological progress and innovation; at the same time we are exhausting scarce natural resources. We produce comfortable cars, but city life is being destroyed, and the number of accidents is increasing. A vast

---

* Lecture presented at the Institute for Christian Studies, Toronto, November 12, 1976.

number of books is being published about every conceivable problem, while the old problems of decades ago are not being solved.

The discrepancy between the ideal of human progress and the reality of life on earth appears to grow increasingly. Each step forward implies a step backward. Professor D. Johnson of the Massachusetts Institute of Technology once characterized this situation by saying that "Technology is both a social benefactor and a social disaster."

The Dutch historian Jan Romein has also called attention to this conflicting nature of societal progress. He even formulated a so-called "law of the braking start" to indicate that each step of progress bears in itself the germs for a reaction. In fact, he regarded the very notion of *progress* to be a dubious concept. For that reason he preferred to use the more neutral term *movement*.

It is of crucial importance for us to get at the root of this discrepancy between progress and backlash. For is not progress "without a human face" in fact a dangerous threat to society, so that progress and future perspective tend to become counter-active forces? And does not modern technology at times play the role of both a social benefactor and a social disaster? Clearly, the expansion of technology during the last decades makes the matter of its harmonious use more urgent, for its potential misuse increases at the same rate.

In view of this, what may we expect with regard to the future? Some claim there is good reason not to be too optimistic, because each human activity seems to bring us further from a paradise on earth. However, it is often argued that there is equally good reason not to be too pessimistic, for precisely technology seems able to lead us back to a paradise on earth.

The dichotomy optimism/pessimism, in my view, is a false one, however. The development of the earth is not a freak of nature fluctuating between good and bad. Nor is it in the hands of fate. On the contrary, the great Creator and Recreator of all things holds the reins of this development. In his Word, He promises that He will not leave us to our fate. We, as God's children, may therefore derive comfort from the firmness of this promise in the face of our present predicament.

I am fully aware that this conviction is religious in nature and cannot be proven by scientific argument. That holds ultimately for all questions about the origin, the meaning, and the future of human existence. Even the well-known atheistic philosopher Jean-Paul Sartre acknowledges this when he implies that ultimately one must surrender either to God or to the absurd.

In addition to the consolation God's children may experience from the knowledge of the Lord's continuing support with regard to future developments of the earth and society, I want to emphasize a second point. The Bible clearly reveals that man is not a passive being; on the contrary, man has been given the responsibility to develop the earth and society in honour of the Lord and for the benefit of his fellow human beings.

It is important to keep in mind that these two starting points constitute the premises of the discussion following below.

## *Historical sketch*

Today western culture seems to be in a state of transition. The expectation of a future with unprecedented possibilities has vanished into thin air. Our welfare state or "affluent society," as Galbraith put it, appears to have a weaker foundation than was assumed in the past. The number of predictions about catastrophes and calamities is increasing rapidly, and doubt about future possibilities is spreading.

This change reflects a reversal in postwar developments and expectations away from the high ideal of progress and economic expansion. The present problems of unemployment, energy shortages, and environmental decay are signs of this sharp contrast.

The economic and technological expansion we have come to expect since the industrial revolution seems to have come to an end. Our welfare state appears unable to realize further quantitative growth. The realization of new growth ambitions in our welfare state will undermine our present and future living conditions.

Hence, technological and economic progress is no longer an indisputable objective. The traditional premise or paradigm of economics—i.e., the principle of *maximization* based on rational and efficient management—is increasingly being attacked. The concept of a basic paradigm in the special sciences was introduced by Thomas S. Kuhn in his famous book entitled *The*

*Structure of Scientific Revolutions.* In this study Kuhn examined the manner in which prevailing fundamental starting points— so-called paradigms—arose and developed. In his opinion, changes in paradigms are an essential element in the evolution of the special sciences because prevailing paradigms lose credibility as society and its external conditions change. Such change requires a new paradigm, so that the problems we face today can be analyzed more adequately. This change in the intellectual basis of a science is called a scientific revolution.

It cannot be denied that the traditional economic paradigm—i.e., the maximization of the gross national product (GNP)—has controlled the development of western society to a considerable extent. The resultant negative external effects, such as energy exhaustion, environmental pollution, and third-world problems, have contributed to serious doubts with respect to this traditional paradigm. A. Coddington, for example, has stated that "Economic growth leads to an obsolescence of many things, and one of these things is economic theory itself."[1]

It is therefore not surprising that at present several scientists are attempting to propose a new paradigm or a new scientific and intellectual cornerstone for economics and the social sciences. Among these belong Kenneth Boulding, Herman Daly, and Nicolas Georgescu-Roegen. The concept of a *steady-state economy* plays a key role in their writings. A steady state does not necessarily imply zero growth; it refers to an economic system characterized by an equilibrium with respect to its scarce resources. The proponents of this new paradigm therefore emphasize the necessity of a greater durability of commodities as well as recycling processes.

In my view, several arguments of the "new paradigm school" are quite convincing. However, the acceptance of a new paradigm as such does not guarantee a definite solution, since it is usually based on tactical and anthropocentric grounds. We have to probe more deeply. As long as we neglect the biblical revelation about man as steward in God's creation with the responsibility to unfold the diverse earthly resources in a harmonious way, only the direction from which the danger comes can be altered but the danger itself remains. Therefore, the new paradigm should be based on the ancient biblical notion of stewardship. This normative starting point certainly does not guarantee a future without problems but it provides a hopeful perspective for our acts and thoughts.

## *Sacredness of growth*

This normative approach to progress and expansion is in sharp contrast with the commonly accepted paradigm of unlimited growth, sometimes called "growth mania." Western society is not the victim of blind fate; it has made a conscious choice in favour of an ideology of expansion.

It cannot be denied that economic and technological growth has had many positive and valuable effects on our society. Medical care, for instance, has markedly improved; the daily comfort of life has benefited most people; and communication has become easier and more accessible. One would expect that these and other results of economic maturity would have led to a great sense of satisfaction and appreciation in the industrialized world. However, it is amazing that discontent has not at all disappeared; instead, it has increased even more rapidly than our material abundance.

The expansion ideology has affected western man to such an extent that growth is considered a right rather than a blessing. Economists will explain this situation by pointing to a widening of people's expectations. As incomes grow, they become aware of more possibilities, so that a rise in income will generate a new rise in wants. In a growing economy this process will continue, at least as long as it is taken for granted that human wants are infinite. It is obvious that the general discontent—itself a result of economic growth—will spread even more quickly when environmental problems—also a result of economic growth—become more serious.

This spiral movement can only be reversed if the assumption of unlimited wants is abandoned—in economic theory, in personal attitudes, and in economic policy making. This is not a tactical move. Expansion ideology with its unlimited wants is, in fact, contrary to the biblical notions of stewardship and moderation. Man is not to be a slave to economic expansion; he is fully responsible for all his activities. Therefore, material progress should never be an end in itself; it should always be related to the service of God and fellow human beings.

Economics is not a neutral science. The acceptance of the

paradigm of maximizing behaviour has provided a theoretical
justification for expansion. It should be emphasized that human
needs and preferences do not lie outside the discipline of
economic theory. It belongs to the task of the science of
economics to raise critical questions about human priorities.
Only then will it be what it ought to be; namely, a search for
responsible and harmonious strategies to be pursued in a world
with finite resources. Otherwise, economics will only be an
"after-the-fact" science which studies primarily the solutions to
bad repercussions of wrong priorities. These repercussions
include the problems of congestion, pollution, energy
exhaustion, and poverty.

The above analysis does not imply that economic growth as
such is bad. It is bad only if it is the consequence of an expansion
ideology in which self-serving materialistic priorities dominate
and in which service to the Lord and fellow human beings is
neglected. This is clearly evident from the New Testament,
where we read "For everything created by God is good, and
nothing is to be rejected if it is received with thanksgiving; for
then it is consecrated by the word of God and prayer."
(I Timothy 4:4-5; R.S.V.)

Further, we should realize that not all economic growth since
the second world war can be attributed to the ideology of
expansion. Growth has frequently been necessary in dealing
with imbalance in income and property, unemployment, and
third-world problems.

Unfortunately, the ideology of expansion has become a
dominant motive in the western world. Many people have
substituted faith in a living God with faith in dead
commodities. Their motto for life is no longer "In God we
trust" but "In Gold we trust." They believe in the "Sacredness
of Growth." The growth thermometer has become the measure
for their earthly state of grace!

It is remarkable that doubts about the future—such as those
expressed by The Club of Rome—did not lead to a reversal of
the expansion ideology. In fact, the opposite occurred. For,
when it became clear that the future paradise on earth was far
hence and perhaps even inaccessible, the ideology of expansion
led to a short-term satisfaction of wants. The guide for life
consequently read: "Let us eat and drink now, for tomorrow we
will die."

## Technology and progress

Actual economic expansion since the second world war was made possible only by technological advance. Since technological advance was regarded to be neutral or a-normative, it was not understood that in effect it served as the vehicle for an irresponsible ideology of economic expansion. For instance, the French scientist Jean Fourastié has stated that technological advance will ultimately lead to a stable economic equilibrium in society in which the tertiary service sector will play a particularly dominant role. This optimistic conception, however, overlooks the negative external effects of technological advance, such as congestion, pollution, depletion of natural resources, and international discrepancies between poor and rich countries.

Technology and science seem to have taken on an existence of their own, increasingly dominating our life. The German philosopher Friedrich von Weiszacker has noted that the universities tend to become the new temples of mankind and scientists the priests. Quite clearly this poses the necessity of a deeper reflection on man's concrete task on earth, since the negative external effects of an unlimited and a-normative technological growth become more and more apparent.

Kenneth Boulding provides an example of such reflection. He has compared the earth with a spaceship which is dependent on input of material—such as food and energy—from the outside. Since the earth's resources are limited and not to be expanded at will by materials from the outside, unlimited growth is impossible. For that reason Boulding advocates a "spaceman economy" instead of the present "cowboy economy." A "cowboy economy" stresses growth in consumption, production, and material waste, whereas a "spaceman economy" stresses responsible use of scarce resources in order to achieve an equilibrium within the earthly ecosystem.

Boulding's idea is worthwhile and appealing but one should be aware of the fact that scarcity and finiteness are *relative,* for the use of scarce resources and their availability are codetermined by their relative prices. Thus, if some materials become too expensive, a search for substitutes will be stimulated. In my opinion, it is a basic task of modern technology not to support

the expansion ideology but to investigate the possibilities of a
more balanced development of the earth. To accomplish such
development, I feel acceptance of the biblical norm of
responsible stewardship is fundamental. This would do away
with the idea of a "spaceship earth" and its spasmodic
recuperation. Unfortunately, Boulding did not understand this
biblical message; in fact, he claims that biblical ethics induces
waste and pollution, because the Bible teaches that there is no
reason to worry about tomorrow. He neglects, however, that
the promise for the future holds only if man takes his task as a
steward on earth seriously. Others, similarly, reject this biblical
mandate. They consider present earthly developments necessary
because there is no other way to overcome the past problems of
poverty. For them human actions are merely adaptations.
However, man is not an impersonal function of an evolutionary
process in which he is only able to react to external challenges, as
is implied by the well-known "challenge and response" theory
of the historian Arnold J. Toynbee. We should remember that
man is a responsible being, charged with the God-given task to
cultivate the earth.

I am convinced that much more could be said. However, this
is a problem for christian anthropology—unfortunately a
frequently neglected field. In my opinion, this must be dealt
with in the foreseeable future, since, as I hope to show later, it is
a necessary condition for the adoption of alternative and
normative ways with respect to the development of the economy
and technology.


## A risky future?

The belief in the realization of an earthly paradise was to a large
extent shattered by the publications of The Club of Rome. The
First Report for The Club of Rome, entitled *The Limits to Growth*
(written by D.H. Meadows *et al.* in 1972), predicted that our
economic and ecological system would collapse within one
century if the present growth spiral continued in the future. On
the basis of a world model (which included demographic
growth, food production, pollution, investments, and
depletion of resources) the future development of the earth was

simulated. Thus a set of conditional calculations was made on the assumption that present trends in production and consumption would continue. These calculations demonstrated that world-wide and large-scale famine, energy exhaustion and environmental pollution could not be avoided in the future.

This report can be criticized form several points of view.

1. The information about food production and available resources is very inaccurate and unreliable.

2. The hypothesis of a one-world system is untenable, because the world consists of many diverse regions with completely different cultural, religious, and socioeconomic backgrounds, and different physical conditions.

3. Little significance is attached to adequate and adjusted technological growth.

4. The price mechanism is neglected; higher prices stimulate economical use and a search for substitutes.

5. The "exponential growth" assumption neglects the possibility of a change in human attitudes.

6. The term *overpopulation* is used without taking into account that this concept is determined by a whole set of factors.

7. The deterministic starting point of a systems theory in which human behaviour is only of a mechanical nature is adopted without question.

8. The emphasis on world planning does not take into account the substantial effects at a local, regional or national level.

In my view, it is a fundamental shortcoming of this study that the richness of God's creation has been overlooked. God created the earth with an enormous potential for development and He has provided mankind with many and diverse talents to cultivate this planet in a harmonious manner.

Nevertheless, the report was very useful in confronting man with the consequences of his choices and actions and with the tensions resulting from his growth ideals.

The Second Report for The Club of Rome, *Mankind at the Turning Point* (written two years later by Mihajlo Mesarović and Eduard Pestel), can be seen as a follow-up to and improvement on the First Report. The conclusions of the Second Report are more or less similar to those of the First, for it is predicted that within fifty years a huge catastrophe on earth will take place, since millions of people will starve to death. The situation on the energy and resource market will also become alarming and will lead to a serious economic crisis.

With respect to three points the Second Report can be considered an improvement over the First Report.

1. The hypothesis of a one-world system has been abandoned; instead, the world has been divided into ten areas (such as North America, Western Europe, etc.) on the assumption that the coming crises may come about in different areas at different times.

2. A hierarchy of different decision-making levels has been assumed.

3. A variety of and possible change in human attitudes are taken into account.

The approach adopted in the second study is similar to that of the first: it is a scenario analysis based on conditional calculations of future trends. The conclusions are more or less comparable: crises and catastrophes!

The main difference between these two reports is that according to the second an escape is possible; for if the whole world would adopt a strategy of so-called *organic* growth, then the future would not be hopeless. This strategy implies the surrender of unlimited growth and the pursuit of a balanced development.

The Second Report can also be criticized on several counts.

1. Changes in human attitudes are acknowledged without reference to motives and norms which shape them.

2. Despite regional divisions, the operational management of the environment, food, etc., on a regional level is not articulated.

3. The only norm adopted for human actions is an anthropocentric survival strategy; but man should also be able to live fifty years from now.

4. The division of the world into ten regions is so global that there is no possibility to formulate a national policy; yet, national policies seem to be the most effective instruments for the moment.

5. The problems of the developing countries are mainly discussed in terms of income discrepancies, food shortages and investment aids; these elements, important as they are, do not reflect the core concerns of the developing world (see below).

6. The potentials of intermediate, small-scale technology and of alternative food sources (such as fishery farms) are overlooked.

It is my conclusion that the Second Report is an important piece of research. However, for above-mentioned reasons, its reliability is still very low. A basic shortcoming is that human well-being is only looked at from the point of view of material welfare and that no attention is paid to the biblical mandate that mankind should be concerned above everything else with the Kingdom of God (Mathew 6:19-23).

On the other hand, this report rightly points out that organic growth is preferable to "cowboy" growth, particularly if we take the situation of the developing countries into account. If it is indeed true that the consumption of our western world precludes the development of the poor nations and even causes the death of many human beings, then it is an urgent matter to question whether our own attitudes with respect to growth and welfare should not change and whether the production of many useless luxury goods should not be stopped. The conditions in cities like Calcutta are indeed terrifying; many people literally starve to death. Is it not tragic that the well-known Sister Theresa is working there, not to keep these people alive, but only to provide them with a decent deathbed? Only a cynic would say: "the death of an individual is dismal; the death of millions is a statistical fact!" We bear indeed a great responsibility!

The future with all its secrets has always preoccupied mankind. Fatalists who predict the end of the western world, like the German historian Oswald Spengler, are succeeded by optimists who believe in the unknown potential of the world, like the neomarxist Ernst Bloch. Fatalism and utopianism spring essentially from the same source; namely, the search for an attitude with respect to an uncertain future. In this context the words of Christ, "I will be with you," sound very comforting to his children. This promise provides a hopeful perspective for all our activities in a broken world. There is light, even if the future seems dark.

Not too long ago the issue of an uncertain future was investigated by Robert L. Heilbroner, well-known American historian of economic theory and practice. In *The Human Prospect* he states that our earthly perspective is probably hopeless. His book contains many predictions about future catastrophes. My primary objection to Heilbroner's treatise is the absence of proof in support of his statements. He does not engage in a thorough-going analysis. At the end of his book he even asserts that extensive arguments are meaningless for those who don't want to accept the basic message of his book. In that regard his book is poor and inadequate.

The one interesting thing it contains is his claim that the forthcoming threats cannot be fought effectively. The existing socioeconomic order is unable to prevent a disaster. A socialistic order might perhaps delay future disasters, but in the long run neither socialism nor capitalism will be able to prevent the ultimate catastrophes.

It seems to me that these statements are inadmissible simplification, for the dichotomy capitalism/socialism is a false one. The number of undiluted capitalist or socialist countries is very limited. There are many states under the influence of both isms. It is of fundamental significance to be aware that the dichotomy capitalism/socialism is unacceptable for a Christian. A christian view of the world and of society may never be identified with capitalism which is based on the individual right of the strongest; nor may it be identified with socialism which is based on collective solidarity without taking individual responsibility into account. It is extremely important to realize that, according to the bible, any economic order should be based on the norms of justice, harmony and love. This starting point is diametrically opposed to the acceptance of capitalism, socialism, or dictatorship as the building block for an authentic order.

It is essential for us as Christians to emphasize that the Bible provides the instruments to test whether a certain order is acceptable or not. Further, it is essential to stress that economic structures, important as they are, may never be considered abstract societal phenomena. In our attempt to provide a critical view of the present economic structures, we may not neglect the call for individual conversion and individual responsibility. This is of particular importance because the ultimate christian hope of the future is not oriented to alternative economic structures for this earth, but to a new heaven and a new earth.

## Christianity and progress

Nowadays it is frequently asked whether Christianity is not a source for man's belief in earthly progress and an earthly paradise. It is certainly true that the christian faith is oriented toward a new future. But this does not concern a future of this earth. The search for an earthly paradise is essentially the result of a humanistic ideology of progress in accordance with which man wants to realize his own paradise by means of rational reflection on and control over reality. However, the pursuit of an enriched future on earth seems to have become more and more impossible. Man's optimistic belief in progress is increasingly being destroyed. His loss of this faith and his resultant disappointment leads us to ask whether a relationship exists between Christianity and progress.

At the beginning of this century, the German sociologist Max Weber launched the hypothesis that Christianity or, more precisely, Calvinism is responsible for the capitalist struggle for economic progress. In his opinion, puritan ethics favoured the rise of capitalism. It is my conviction that this thesis cannot be proven. In the first place, puritan theology is not representative of calvinist theology; secondly, despite this, key statements made by many puritan theologians do not support the weberian thesis; thirdly, the doctrine of predestination is central to Calvin's theology and its acceptance does not lead to doubt or to a restless search for material gain; fourthly, a brazen merchant's mentality which determines capitalist success cannot be reconciled with the calvinist ethics of love for the poor and the weak; finally, in many countries a whole complex of factors has played a significant role in the rise of capitalism.

Calvinist ethics is an outgrowth of biblical norms while capitalism is an outgrowth of the Enlightenment. In my opinion, they are, therefore, counteractive instead of mutually supportive forces.

It is both surprising and disappointing that Christianity, in many modern publications, is considered to be the main source of western progress. In earlier centuries Christianity was considered the enemy of science, since it supposedly provided no room for free scientific research and renewal (cf. Darwin and Galileo). During the Enlightenment, for example, Christianity was accused of shortsightedness because it deprived man of his autonomous intellect by submitting it to the will of God. Today, however, it is openly proclaimed that Christianity stimulated technological and economic progress to such a degree that in the future the earth even runs the risk of being destroyed. In other words, Christianity receives both the credit and the blame for progress and its power of destruction.

As I have tried to demonstrate, these arguments cannot be justified. I want to add, however, that Christianity has often given rise to many mistakes. As Christians we should, therefore, not be proud of ourselves, but should continually take a critical look at our actions in the light of the Bible.

## Biblical responsibility

Several times so far, I mentioned the word *responsibility* as a key word in christian ethics. What does this word mean? Responsibility is derived from the word *response.* In essence this means that man has to give the right response to the call and norms of God's Word. In other words, reponsibility does not refer to man's autonomous activity; to the contrary, it is an echo of the Bible.

I am fully aware that the word *responsibility* as such is a rather loose concept. Therefore, I would like to make it more transparent by discussing it in the context of five basic starting points.

1. A responsible and obedient Christian never looks at nature with contempt or regards it as a source for unlimited exploitation, since it is part of God's creation. Against the light of the Bible, nature receives relief in which one recognizes the act of the Creator himself. This starting point has obvious repercussions for man's responsible choice in consumption, production, and recreation.

2. Responsibility refers to stewardship in a concrete situation, confined to a certain time span. It limits one's obligation with regard to the future and implies a less spasmodic attitude with regard to long-term future problems. Christian stewardship is

related to concrete situations in which one can carry out one's present responsibility.

3. To illustrate one concrete situation, the finiteness of the earth's resources requires stewardly concern for maximal preservation. Technology and economics should therefore be geared to the responsible use of energy and raw materials. International discrepancies in energy consumption, for instance, should be reduced in order to create more development opportunities for poor countries.

4. Labour is not an end in itself or a means to achieve maximum wealth. Labour is a means to support life, to develop the earth in a harmonious manner and to help one's neighbour. It is not a "necessary evil" (disutility), or a cost factor in a production process; it is a means to carry out the command to act responsibly and adequately.

5. Responsible stewardship takes into account the conditions of poor people, even when they are far away. Third-world problems should not be neglected in our thoughts and acts.

To pay more attention in this context to the concrete and societal implications of these starting points for a christian view of and attitude toward the world would require too much time and space. In my book *Naar een maatschappij zonder toekomst?* [Toward a society without a future?] (Groningen, The Netherlands: De Vuurbaak, 1976), I devoted an entire chapter to such issues as a new lifestyle, the ethics of labour and employment, the management of the environment, our physical space and energy resources, the present socioeconomic order, and the third world. An adequate discussion of the problems facing the developing countries by itself would require a great deal of space. For the complexity of these problems is all too often overlooked in our western way of thinking and living.

It is extremely difficult to give a reliable operational description of a poor country. In my opinion, poverty is not only a matter of low income; more fundamentally, it exists when the biblical basis for the support of life can no longer be fulfilled adequately in various areas of man's existence. In other words, a description of poverty takes into account the aforementioned central concept of christian responsibility.

It is a near impossibility to describe the course of under-development in just a few words. This can be attributed largely to the complexity of the situation, since it is affected by cultural, religious, historical, social, economic, and many other factors. However, it cannot be denied that at present the possibility for development in many countries is hampered by the position of economic power on the part of the rich nations. This can easily be demonstrated, for instance, by statistical figures for grain sold by the West.

It is clear that a solution to the problem of underdevelopment can only be found in a two-fold strategy. First, the western world should take its responsibility toward the poor nations more seriously by creating an international economic structure which favours not the powerful countries but the poorer ones. In my view, christian responsibility as set out above is also of crucial relevance in attacking the problem of underdevelopment.

Secondly, the poor nations should also take their task seriously. Educational facilities, agricultural reforms, construction of infrastructural facilities, and so forth, will only bear fruit if the rich are prepared to help and cooperate with the poor. This is a huge problem for both, but it is also a huge challenge. Further, it should be kept in mind that the problems facing the poor countries in general do not constitute a lack of food or knowledge, but a lack of communication, of a right distribution of resources and food, and of a stable and effective social infrastructure.

The late E. F. Schumacher made some very important proposals in his interesting book, *Small is Beautiful,* to help solve the problems of underdevelopment. In his opinion, efforts toward small-scale development by means of which poor people become involved in the employment process are much more effective than huge industrialization programs which require specialized labourers. The masses can be helped only by the development of rural areas and by a reduction in the flight to the big cities. It seems to me that the so-called intermediate technology he advocates bears a striking resemblance to the way in which the christian missions have worked, i.e., by starting off in small places and trying to develop from there into a larger area.

So far, I have not discussed the task of christian missions. It would be a mistake to believe that preaching the Holy Scriptures would automatically solve the problem of underdeveloped areas; there still are many underdeveloped christian regions. It would also be a mistake to believe that missions have nothing to do with underdevelopment. It is a necessary prerequisite for the improvement of underdeveloped areas that the notion of christian responsibility is kept alive. But a real danger exists that contemporary christian missions will only preach a social gospel, or even a neomarxist gospel, which severely criticizes the socioeconomic structures of a poor nation without reference to the biblical call to conversion and promise of redemption. Conversion and redemption are of crucial relevance for both East and West, North and South, as well as for individuals and groups.

The church—not as an abstract entity, but as a concrete gathering of God's children—has indeed an enormous task in our world. It must emphasize that there is a future for our world. This will not be a paradise on earth, but a future which transcends this earth and will include both rich and poor. This promise may stimulate us to continue our work, even if we doubt the effectiveness of some of our efforts. There is a task for everyone and we may rest assured that the value of our christian contribution is not dependent on the quantity but on the normative quality of our activities. Our faith in the promise that in Christ Jesus we are the inheritors of a new future also opens a window onto the infinite perspective of the present.


*Note*

1. A.Coddington, "The Economics of Ecology," *New Society*, 4 April 1970, p. 596.

# 6 *From Confrontation to Partnership*[*]

*by Harry Antonides*

The Christian Labour Association of Canada (CLAC) has consistently advocated the need to fundamentally challenge the adversary system, and to replace it with one in which the contributions of labour and management are seen as a cooperative effort.

## *Introduction*

Ever since its founding in 1952, the CLAC—with affiliated locals operating as certified unions in Alberta, British Columbia, and primarily in Ontario—has worked hard at putting its ideas into practice. The going has not been easy, but a beginning has been made in raising a different voice and in showing that labour

---

[*] *Revised version of a submission to the Minister of Labour made by the CLAC in May 1977.*

relations need not be paternalistic nor revolutionary. The purpose of this article is to highlight the main areas where, according to the CLAC, fresh thinking and a new approach to labour-management relations is now a priority.

To understand its approach, it is relevant to summarize that the CLAC:

1. Is committed to the christian faith and accepts the Bible as the norm for human relations.

2. Believes that labour-management relations are, or ought to be , cooperative relationships, although the need to differentiate with respect to responsibility and authority should be acknowledged.

3. Views work as a meaningful task for the purpose of developing talents, enjoying the resources of creation and interacting with one another.

4. Considers the enterprise a work community in which various participants, including entrepreneurs, managers, tradesmen, professional and other workers, engage in meaningful work to meet the genuine needs of society with the supply of goods and services.

5. Considers freedom of religion and freedom of association indispensible building blocks of an open (free) society.

6. Favours societal pluralism and opposes artificial uniformity.

7. Advocates a sense of stewardship with respect to natural resources and the environment.

8. Acknowledges Canada's coresponsibility for the proper political, social and economic development of other nations, especially those belonging to the so-called third world.

Today a growing uneasiness about the state of labour relations in Canada is clearly evident. On the one hand, there is continuing reliance on the adversary method in collective bargaining with its bread-and-butter emphasis, its ceaseless demand for "more." The prospects of this focus are dismal. On the other hand, voices advocating a new, more cooperative relationship between management and workers are becoming louder. Invariably, attention turns to forms of codetermination existing in various European countries. For example, in 1978, professor John Crispo published a study on the collective bargaining system of all major West European countries with a view to acquaint labour and management in Canada with alternatives to the adversary approach. In the introduction, Crispo writes that the "fundamental issue is whether collective bargaining as it has been traditionally practiced in North America can survive." Another study dealing with European labour relations, commissioned in 1975 by the Canada Department of Labour, is Charles Connaghan's study of industrial democracy in Germany. It is significant to note its subtitle:

> A critical examination of contemporary labour-relations in West Germany with suggestions for improving the Canadian labour-management relationships based on the West German experience.

In May 1977 the federal Department of Labour, spurred by the desire to phase out Canada's wage-and-price control program, issued a brochure entitled "A Better Work Environment for Canadians" which contained a series of suggestions for the development of a more cooperative approach to collective bargaining. This publication stresses the need to make work itself more rewarding and meaningful and to develop more consultation between labour and management. It became the specific occasion for the CLAC to address the Minister of Labour in an open letter, pointing to some of the underlying causes of the unsatisfactory state of affairs in industrial relations, and commenting on the suggestions the brochure made to improve the work environment and the labour-relations system.

## Roots of current labour problems

The CLAC welcomes all attempts to improve relationships between workers and management and wants to contribute to this development. It would be a mistake to think, as many do, that the present collective bargaining system is basically sound and needs merely a number of procedural and technical adjustments. These are needed but, more importantly, attention must be paid to the roots of the present crisis in Canadian labour relations. Demanded is a fundamental critique

of the idea that labour-management relations are essentially
adversarial in nature. This will require a great deal of careful
thought and deliberate restructuring, because the ideas
undergirding the adversary notion are deeply imbedded in
contemporary society. They include the following premises:

1. Man is first of all an individual entitled to look after his own
interests as a priority item.

2. The corporation is an entity in which the growth of profit and
size is the primary goal.

3. Labour unions are expressions of the collective self-interest of
the workers, and are entitled to gain maximum benefits for their
members.

4. Society is made up of a collection of competing interests
which must be kept in some kind of equilibrium.

5. The good life consists of a growing amount of consumer
goods and leisure time, realizable via the ever-expanding gross
national product.

A number of simultaneous distortions—especially inflation
and unemployment—in economic, social, and political
structures, accompanied by a declining faith in democracy, has
given rise to a measure of doubt about these five premises. The
danger is real that a growing sense of frustration and
helplessness will lead to complete cynicism and loss of
confidence in the viability of a free society. In counteracting
that possibility, the CLAC feels compelled to challenge the five
premises listed above and to urge others, especially those in
leadership positions, to engage in fundamental analysis and
restructuring rather than apply bandaids here and there. A few
comments about each of the five points are in order.


## 1. *The leading role of individualism*

Many people today would refute Adam Smith's dictum that
self-interest is the motor of economic activity and progress.
Nonetheless, this notion is still powerfully present in our time.
The belief in individualism is somewhat hedged in and
safeguarded against its extreme and logical conclusions, but we
have in no way succeeded in undercutting the idea that the
individual is entitled to pursue his own interests as a matter of

principle. It comes to expression in many ways, perhaps most strikingly in the way advertising exploits man's self-image and status.

The opposite of individualism—namely, collectivism—at first sight appears to be an acceptable antidote but, in reality, it does not remove the evil of the former. Instead of absolutizing the individual, collectivism absolutizes the community; in both instances the stifling of genuine personality and wholesome human relationships is the outcome.

In the light of biblical revelation we must conclude that absolutization of the individual or the collective has to be rejected in favour of a normative view of man. This starting point entails the acknowledgment that man is created in the image of God, made to serve his Creator and live in fellowship with others. Instead of pursuing self-interest, man is to respond to the biblical norms of justice, love, and stewardship. These norms place social relations and economic activity in a very different light from that which is prominent today.

### 2. *Goals of the business enterprise*

The spirit of self-interest has become the dominant principle on which economic activity and the business enterprise are built. The modern corporation has become seriously distorted because of its preoccupation with the interests of those who provide capital. As a consequence, economic and technical goals have become preeminent. Ongoing growth of the business enterprise, rather than all-round enrichment of human life, has become the purpose of production and marketing. The result of this onesided concern is a preoccupation with efficiency in the workplace at the expense of social and environmental well-being.

The modern production system has led to a loss of meaningful, rewarding, and socially stimulating work. By and large the worker has been reduced to a factor of production. This point has been belaboured by many observers and experts. It should be noted that the present upsurge of concern and the suggestions for change are generally accompanied by the assurance that "humanization" of work will at the same time enhance productivity. This may be the case in certain instances, but we should be prepared to suffer a setback in productivity if that is needed to make the workplace an environment in which people can again thrive as responsible persons. We may be required to sacrifice productivity in order to bring about the modifications needed to restore workers to a place of responsibility in their work. It will be impossible to bring about fundamental changes in the workplace unless we are prepared to challenge prevailing beliefs about the purpose of work and the role of the corporation.

The foregoing is all the more imperative in view of the present trend toward more capital- and energy-intensive, labour-saving, and technologically complex investment. This implies the irresponsible use of scarce resources, and contributes to the stuctural distortions of severe unemployment and inflation.

The corporation is generally viewed as a technical, legal entity in which the suppliers of capital possess all the rights of management. But it is first of all a structure in which human beings form a *work community*. To be sure, division of tasks and diversity in authority and responsibility must be respected. Management needs room and authority to manage. At the same time, all persons involved in an enterprise should be regarded as fully human, as beings who in their own work must be able to realize something of the responsibility and the challenge that has been accorded to them by the Creator.

### 3. *Labour unions: expressions of collective self-interest*

Unions have accepted their role generally without challenging the assumptions mentioned above. They view themselves as power centres that must safeguard the interests of their members by obtaining the maximum slice of the economic pie. Consequently, collective bargaining has deteriorated into a cynical struggle for power in which the norm of justice is trampled underfoot. This was stated in so many words by a prominent trade unionist, as follows:

> And, having real power, they [unions] would be foolish not to exercise it. Power, after all, is really what collective bargaining in Canada is all about—not justice, or ability, or merit, but naked power. (Ed Finn, *The Toronto Star,* January 24, 1972.)

The result is that those unions which muster enough power are able to squeeze the most out of the system. A host of examples exists of this *selfish* motive of many trade unions. The

so-called jurisdictional disputes that sometimes occur in the
construction industry clearly illustrate this mentality. What
dominates in such wasteful and silly conflicts is not the genuine
interests of working people, but the relative power of unions in
terms of numbers, money, and job control.

One of the pernicious results of the adversary system is that
the real problems in the workplace, stemming from failure to
view and treat the worker as a responsible human—i.e.,
social—being, are ignored. Instead, the raising of wages and
the reduction in hours of work have become the overriding
objectives of unions. What we need is new directions in
collective bargaining. For that reason the current interest in
improving the work environment is a positive sign.

4. *Society as a battleground of competing interests*

Another serious obstacle to a normative development is the
notion that society consists of a collection of interest groups
related to one another in a competitive way, each striving to
satisfy its own interest. In this context the state is seen as the
traffic controller, to make sure that the imbalance of power
among the various groups does not get out of hand. A set of rules
and procedures are thought to be sufficient to somehow contain
the ongoing struggle between the various interest groups, while
a system of lobbying is used to oil the machinery.

The basic trouble with this conception is that self-interest
and greed are very difficult, if not impossible, to contain. The
tendency will always be that the powerful abuse their power at
the expense of the weak. The government finds itself in an
extremely difficult position since, on the one hand, it is
subjected to a great deal of pressure from those who can exert
influence while, on the other, it seeks to be a protective shield
for those who are most in need. This is a dilemma which cannot
be resolved. Until now a complete breakdown of our society has
been staved off partly because the regularly growing gross
national product enabled most groups in society to enhance
their own position. However, the limits of natural resources and
other restraints are bound to put a stop to an ever-growing GNP.
This has been driven home especially after the OPEC countries
imposed staggering increases in the price of oil. As a result, we
are now faced with a more acute social crisis than we realized
before. This is apparent from rising inflation and

unemployment, and, in a more fundamental way, from the ongoing decline in mutual trust and tolerance. It is obvious that confrontation tactics between various groupings in our society are becoming increasingly popular. Canada's deplorable strike record is an indication of this. Growing tensions between government and citizens, the separatist movement in Quebec, mounting disagreements between the federal government and the provinces, and among the various regions of Canada, are all symptoms of a disease that will not go away by wishful thinking or procedural tinkering.

The 1976 Manifesto of the Canadian Labour Congress advocated tripartite sharing of power between government, business, and labour. This proposal is the outcome of the conviction that society consists of a number of interest (or power) blocs. But the direction advocated by the CLC will lead to a corporatist society in which there will not be room for societal plurality and freedom. In contrast to that, CLAC favours an open society in which the variety and multiplicity of beliefs, structures, and organizations are recognized and respected. It is our conviction that the biblical view of man and the biblical norm for human relationships provide a perspective that will be eminently helpful in working toward the growth and preservation of an open and responsible society, precisely because the biblical emphasis is on serving and sharing.

### 5. *The "Good Life"*

Although there has been some rethinking about the assumption that more and bigger is better, this belief is still one of the most powerful forces at work in our society. Moreover, it is thought that man can find fulfilment in self-determination (freedom). That conviction was at the heart of the Enlightenment and lies at the foundation of the idea of progress. Progress implies man's ever-growing mastery over nature; today it is epitomized by possession of consumption goods and leisure time.

Preoccupation with the good life thus narrowly understood has led to a mad pursuit of economic growth and the exhaustion of nonrenewable resources. It has also given rise to many social, political, and economic distortions in the form of severe disparities in income, serious continuous inflation and unemployment, as well as a pervading sense of malaise, frustration, and animosity.

To regard economic growth as the sure road to greater happiness is especially irresponsible in the light of existing disparities between rich and poor nations. A more responsible lifestyle in terms of use of resources and food becomes all the more imperative in view of the reality that millions of people are forced to live at a subsistence level. Our economic priorities must be reconsidered as a matter of social justice. It is totally irresponsible for Canada, as a relatively wealthy nation, to act as if the misery in other parts of the world is of no concern to it. Every price increase of Canadian goods adds to the burden of the poor nations who desperately need Canadian products. This fact is completely ignored by all interest groups preoccupied with themselves.

To bring about lasting improvements in collective bargaining in Canada will, on the one hand, require insight into the complexity of the situation; on the other, it will require a willingness to give and to share, even to sacrifice in some instances, so that the needy can be helped. There are true needs in the work situation, and there are real injustices—all of which must be tackled. But they can be tackled only if we are prepared to raise basic questions and engage in self-criticism. As long as we are unwilling to change our selfish beliefs and aspirations, and as long as each interest group tries to maximize its own advantages, we will fail in improving the collective-bargaining system.

## The quality of working life

The CLAC is of the conviction that the central challenge in the workplace is the restoration of the worker to a place of responsibility in his work. That must take place at two distinct levels: 1) in the office, on the shop floor, at the construction site, or wherever actual work takes place; and 2) within the decision-making process of the enterprise.

### 1. Codetermination in the workplace

The worker is generally viewed as a cost factor within the production system and, for that reason, work is organized as rationally and as efficiently as possible. This developed especially under the particularly pernicious influence of the so-called scientific-management approach, according to which efficiency and profits are supreme. This led to an organization of work and a production system which were based on abstract and rational principles, without regard for authentic norms that hold for work and human interaction. That situation provided fertile soil for the adversary mentality. Today's appeals of management for worker responsibility in terms of performance, and restraint in terms of the limits of the economic system, often fall on deaf ears because earlier management had done everything possible to relieve workers of responsibility and involvement. Exactly at this point new directions must be found. When proper restructuring of work leads to greater productivity, it should certainly be welcomed. However, restructuration should not be made dependent on increased productivity. If, to enhance the position of the workers, certain improvements result in greater economic cost, we may have to be prepared to change our priorities in favour of improvement of the human situation rather than profitability of the operation. At the same time, it cannot be denied that certain companies may consequently face considerable difficulties which must be dealt with. To help alleviate these and to assist such organizations in introducing costly changes that will improve the work situation, consideration could be given to such innovations as preferential tax treatment or the provision of special funds.

The aim must be to enlarge the use of skills, judgment and responsibility in work. This means that, for instance, the trend toward specialization and division of tasks must be halted in favour of job enrichment, variety, and teamwork. Instead of maximizing the role of management and supervision, it should be minimized and revamped to encourage workers to assume more responsibility in the making of decisions on the job. Tasks should be designed to provide an opportunity for workers to enjoy a sense of achievement. Possibilities for social interaction (teamwork) must be expanded. What this adds up to is a rejection of the principles of rationality, and of the scientific approach to organization of work, in favour of a recognition of workers as responsible human beings.

The implementation of this new approach to work could take place through enterprise councils or committees which assume responsibility for workers' involvement in decision making

with respect to the organization of work, including the
introduction of new technologies, work restructuration and job
enrichment. Where unions hold representation rights, they
would naturally play a leading role in the establishment of such
councils, but the tasks of these councils should be expanded
much beyond the traditional scope of trade unions. It will be
difficult to avoid some overlap in task and consequent rivalry
and competition—all of which will hamstring the functioning
of both the enterprise councils and the unions. For that reason it
might be sensible to assign the task of industry-wide collective
bargaining primarily to unions, while enterprise councils could
be expected to concentrate especially on the work group at the
local level.

We must also distinguish between the union's role as a
partner with management in the decision-making process, and
as a defender of workers' rights, sometimes "over against"
management, such as in the handling of grievances. Union fear
of loss of identity and independence is legitimate. This threat
must be anticipated and counteracted as much as possible, for
precisely such fear causes many trade unionists to seek security
in maintaining their adversary role. The difficulties are complex
at this point. For how can a union avoid losing its independence
as an organization which must protect the well-being of its
members if, at the same time, the workers become partners with
management and thus coresponsible for the managerial
decisions? No simple solution to this problem exists, and a great
deal of patience and determination will be required. Perhaps the
answer lies in a recognition of and provision for the two distinct
functions of the union—namely, its representative role on
behalf of its members and its coresponsible role together with
management. (The separation of legislative, judicial, and
executive functions of the government may provide a helpful
analogy here.) What we need is a permanent arbitration and
adjudication body which is to decide in cases of deadlocked
disputes, including deadlocked negotiations. Serious thought
must be given to the establishment of some kind of labour
court.

All of this suggests that we need further refinement of
functions and tasks within the workplace to escape the present
dilemmas that are obviously intolerable and desperately need
imaginative leadership. It is for this reason that a number of

attempts, including those of the federal government, to improve the work situation should be welcomed. It would be unrealistic to expect radical change overnight, but it is imperative that we begin to introduce new ways with a view toward fundamental change in the long run.

### 2. *Codetermination at the top*

As the CLAC has advocated in a number of briefs and submissions to various governmental bodies, it favours a form of codetermination whereby, perhaps gradually, employee representatives begin to assume coresponsibility for the decisions affecting the enterprise. Thus, the CLAC has recommended that legislation be enacted which stipulates that employees as well as shareholders obtain the right to elect persons to the boards of directors of corporations beyond a certain size—those, for instance, with at least one hundred employees. The aim should be parity, but this could be achieved gradually. A representation formula of one-third shareholders, one-third employees, and one-third outsiders acceptable to the shareholders and employees seems to have certain advantages.

We must not only seek structural changes; we should also strive to establish a better relationship between labour and management, so that the atmosphere in which structural changes can take place becomes marked by trust and goodwill rather than by suspicion and antagonism. It is especially for this reason that better relationships in the workplace must be established, in order that workers concretely begin to experience the benefits of the new directions.

## *Improving the collective bargaining system*

The CLAC has consistently advocated the need to overcome the obviously harmful fragmentation which now plagues industrial relations. Fragmentation has been detrimental to the bargaining process, and has resulted in competition among unions, unjustified disparity in wage rates, and even strikes. An additional disadvantage of the present collective bargaining system is the difference between the organized and unorganized sectors.

Industry-wide bargaining—on a regional, provincial, or

federal basis, depending on circumstances—is necessary to bring about a greater measure of equity and fairness. Here the role of the government is obviously paramount. Also, unions need to coordinate and combine efforts in the establishment of collective agreements and in other activities. Greater emphasis has to be placed on cooperation and coordination. Collective bargaining must become more "centralized," and the basic provisions of collective agreements should be extended to the entire industry to which they apply.

Although more centralization and greater uniformity in working conditions and wages is needed, the potential harm of this scheme should be discerned. To avoid the danger of dictatorship, the collective-bargaining system must remain "open," so that minority unions and groups are not excluded. With regard to the use of compulsion by many unions, it is obvious that deliberate measures are needed to ensure that the anticipated centralized structure of collective bargaining will allow for pluriformity and variety. An absolute application of the majoritarian principle would be disastrous.

Freedom of choice in union membership must be safeguarded because there is a direct relationship between men's convictions with respect to ultimates (basic belief or life view) and their view of work, human relations, and the role of a labour union. It makes a great deal of difference whether one is committed to a marxist, pragmatic, or christian view of life—to mention just three possibilities. Each of these commitments will inspire a different understanding of work and human relations at the job. It is an error to believe that such differences can be ignored, and that some kind of "melting-pot," neutral trade union is acceptable to all workers. Instead, CLAC advocates a situation in which the independence and integrity of each different life view and organization is respected, while at the same time a measure of tolerance and willingness to cooperate with others is maintained. This is a minimum requirement for a healthy and open society.

While CLAC defends fundamental freedom of association, it does not favour "freeloading." All workers have an obligation to share the burden and cost of employee representation. Therefore, it is fair that all workers be required to pay a basic amount for that purpose, but only if full freedom of choice is

protected. This can be done 1) by leaving the final choice of
which union to support to each individual worker; that is, by
requiring each employee to pay dues to the union that has the
bargaining rights, provided that those workers who are strongly
committed to a different union can allocate their dues to the
union of their choice; 2) by respecting the convictions of
those who are conscientiously opposed to *all* unions, by
allowing them to contribute an equal amount to a recognized
Canadian charity. In this manner, the twin evils of selfishness
and compulsion can be countered in a fair and responsible way.


## *Summary and conclusion*

On the basis of its christian commitment, the CLAC is convinced
that drastic changes in the collective bargaining system are
needed. Such changes must be enacted in the light of a
fundamental rethinking of prevailing beliefs and assumptions.
There is a great deal of variety and difference among us with
respect to the ultimate questions of life. The greatest challenge
before us is to find a way in which the unity of our political,
economic, and social framework on a national basis is
maintained, while the possibilities for variety in commitment
and lifestyle are safeguarded. This is no easy assignment, and a
growing number of people despair of the possibility to realize
these two aims simultaneously. CLAC refuses to despair, but it
pleads for a fundamental rethinking and thoroughgoing
discussion aimed at overcoming the present difficulties.

What is urgently needed is a national, consultative,
multipartite forum, consisting of representatives from various
sectors of our nation who would jointly formulate ideas and
recommendations to assist government policy makers. (This
was recommended by the federal Minister of Labour in 1977.)
This body should not have decision-making power; emphasis
should be on its stature and level of competence. That's why
appointments to such a forum should not in the first place be
determined by representation—though that cannot be entirely
ignored—but the greatest weight should be given to insight
and competence of the nominees.

Our nation has come to a difficult and critical stage of

development. Which way will it go? It can move further in the direction of confrontation and disintegration. Or it can choose the direction of bureaucracy, control, and centralization, marked by disappearance of variety and freedom. A third way is to engage in fundamental and principled analysis and discussion about priorities. Our aim should be a society in which the unity of as well as the variety within our nation can be expressed. Primary recognition must be given to principles of stewardship, love, and justice, so that a free and open society can flourish in which especially the needs of the poor, the weak, and the minorities are protected. It is with that goal in mind that the CLAC wishes to make its contribution to the development of Canadian society in general and of industrial relations in particular.

# *Contributors*

*Harry Antonides* is Director of Research and Education for the Christian Labour Association of Canada. Before assuming his present position in the Toronto office, he was stationed at the Vancouver office of the CLAC as western Canada's representative, engaging in collective bargaining in British Columbia and Alberta. He serves on the editorial committee of *The Guide,* official organ of the CLAC, and has contributed many substantial articles and book reviews. His most recent publication is entitled *Multinationals and the Peaceable Kingdom* (Toronto: Clarke, Irwin, 1978). His contribution to *A Christian Union in Labour's Wasteland* (Toronto: Wedge, 1978) reads "CLAC— Anachronism or Alternative."

*Sander Griffioen* studied at the Free University of Amsterdam, where he completed the Ph.D. requirements both in the field of economics and in philosophy. He wrote a dissertation on Hegel. In 1976 he came to Canada to assume the position of Senior Member in economic theory and social philosophy at the Institute for Christian Studies in Toronto. Having returned to the Netherlands in the summer of 1979, he teaches social philosophy at the Free University and occupies a special chair in reformational philosophy at the University of Leyden.

*Paul Marshall* teaches political philosophy at Atkinson College, York University, Toronto, and does research for the Committee for Justice and Liberty Foundation (CJL), Toronto. He has published articles on vocation, Puritanism, John Locke, statistical theory, and philosophy of science. He holds a B.Sc. and M.Sc. from the University of Manchester, England, and an

M.A. and Ph.D. from York University. Effective September
1980 he has been appointed as lecturer in political theory at the
Institute for Christian Studies in Toronto.

*Peter Nijkamp* was educated in economics at the Erasmus
University in Rotterdam. Since 1975 he has been full professor
of regional economics at the Free University in Amsterdam. In
addition to articles and books in the field of regional economics,
he also published in the area of a christian view of environmental
management, economics, and labour ethics.

*Edward Vanderkloet* has engaged in extensive collective-
bargaining activities for the CLAC before he became its national
Executive Secretary. He is Editor-in-Chief of *The Guide* and, in
addition to incisive editorials, frequently contributes major
articles as well as lucid book reviews. He serves on the editorial
committee of the *Vanguard,* a bimonthly christian journal.
"Toward a New Social Order" was published in *A Christian
Union in Labour's Wasteland.*

# Index of Persons